Ashes to Ashes

The rise, fall and rise of ENGLISH CRICKET

Ashes to Ashes

The rise, fall and rise of ENGLISH CRICKET

KEITH FLETCHER

AND

IVO TENNANT

headline

First published in 2005
by HEADLINE BOOK PUBLISHING

1

A CIP catalogue record for this title is available from the British Library

ISBN 0 7553 1382 8

Typeset by Palimpsest Book Production Limited,
Polmont, Stirlingshire
Text design by Ben Cracknell Studios
Printed and bound in Great Britain by
Mackays of Chatham plc, Chatham, Kent

Headline's policy is to use papers that are natural, renewable
and recyclable products and made from wood grown in sustainable forests.
The logging and manufacturing processes are expected to conform to the
environmental regulations of the country of origin.

HEADLINE BOOK PUBLISHING
A division of Hodder Headline
338 Euston Road
London NW1 3BH

www.headline.co.uk
www.hodderheadline.com

To Tara and Sarah – for putting
up with me!

C O N T E N T S

by Mike Atherton

This autobiography of one of English cricket's most loyal and highly regarded men is long overdue. I suppose it is fitting that it is to be published during an Australian summer, the Ashes being a thread that ran through Keith's cricketing life: from his role in the Ashes-winning team of 1970-71 under Ray Illingworth; to his battles in 1974-75 against the terrifying Lillee and Thomson, and then on to the rather one-sided series in 1993 and 1995 that contributed to his tenure as England coach being a relatively short one. It is fitting, too, because this year for the first time in many years England have a real chance of winning the Ashes. Should they do so, Keith's influence on players (Graham Gooch and Nasser Hussain to name two), who did so much to haul English cricket back up to where it belongs, should not be underestimated.

My appreciation, I'm afraid, must begin almost at the point at which Keith finished his career. I did see him play in the late 1980s at Fenner's, where he led Essex in their annual match against Cambridge University. But by that time, a combination of a slow pitch, even slower bowlers and his vice-like bottom-handed grip resulted in an innings that I am sure he and the sparse crowd that day have already forgotten. So, I cannot add anything to his reputation as a fine batsman, especially against spin. I don't really need to because it is there in black and white: 37,665 first-class runs in a career spanning 26 years is testament enough to his longevity and excellence.

I really got to know Keith for the first time in 1990 when he coached an England 'A' team to whom I had been appointed vice-captain. Keith's earthy tone and prosaic humour contrasted sharply with the captain, MCJ Nicholas. It was a combination which worked, however, and I quickly began to appreciate Keith's knowledge of the game, a knowledge that belied an often shambling exterior.

Promotion was not far off - for both of us - and Keith became England's second full-time coach after the retirement of Mickey Stewart. Can any coach have had a tougher start - India away and a rampant, Shane Warne-inspired Australia at home? It was a time, more generally, when other teams, through greater professionalism, had caught us up and moved on, while England stood still, rooted forever in history and tradition. There were few of the structural advantages then that the England team enjoy today and so, for Keith, it was very much a case of right coach, wrong time. Despite our rocky fortunes I came to have the utmost respect for Keith as a coach and as a person. Later, I was to say - and still say - that he was one of only a handful that I could trust absolutely during my time as England captain.

What were his qualities? He has a deep knowledge of the game, for sure; a tactical grasp bettered by few, and an inner toughness that enabled him to dismiss the tabloid taunts and criticisms with dignity. (I remember the *Sun* newspaper instructing its readers to send Keith their opinions after one particularly bad day in Australia in 1995. 'Don't worry, Michael,' he said to me, 'I'm tougher than all of them.') He has a particular empathy with younger players and is, I think, the best judge of a young cricketer that I have come across. He would, even now, make a marvellous selector.

And weaknesses? He was, I suppose, innately conservative at a time when cricket was becoming a more aggressive game through the exploits of the all-conquering Australians. He was never at his best in press conferences, but then who is? His biggest weakness, and for those of us who came to know him well it was a constant source of amusement, was his inability to remember names. So, Derek Pringle was introduced to an Indian dignitary as 'Ignall', and 'Ignall' he remains. Eric Clapton was dismissed as 'Ernie Clapham' and at a selection meeting before the West Indies tour in 1994 Keith announced that he wanted 'Martin McCaddick' in the squad. Did he mean Martin McCague or Andrew Caddick? Caddick got the nod, but we shall never know!

If the Ashes has been a constant theme throughout Keith's cricketing life, I think that loyalty has been the theme by which he has lived his life. Despite his shoddy treatment at the hands of the selectors when he was relieved of the England captaincy, and despite being told over the phone that his England coaching days were over, you will never hear Keith utter a bad word about what happened. And still he remains loyal to Essex - a club to whom he has given his working life. He is held in great paternal affection by the players he captained at Essex - and a thumbs up from your peers is usually the soundest judgement of all.

Such loyalty plays well in sport and with sportsmen. It is a shame that the England team he coached a decade ago did not have the advantages enjoyed by those playing now, otherwise Keith would have had a chance to put his abilities and loyalty to better effect. Who knows, then we might have been talking about Keith and not Duncan being the Fletcher who helped to restore England's fortunes.

INTRODUCTION

A professional sportsman is riven by insecurities. He is chosen, dropped and reinstated on the whim of a selector or manager. His position in the team is subject to competition for places, poor form, injury and capricious umpiring, and yet this is a way of life that is a calling. Although I was enthusiastic about other sports, I grew up wanting only to be a cricketer. Nothing could have concentrated my mind more on achieving first-class status and making a living from the game than the grinding existence I encountered in the East End of London, where I was living in a bedsit at the age of 16. The rag and bone man in Bethnal Green and the customers of the pie and mash shops provided stark images of what might befall if I did not succeed. I had left school and home to try to forge a career with Essex and had no educational qualifications to my name, or family money. There was no guidance on what I should do in the winter months or, worse, if I failed to make any runs.

Throughout a long career in county and international cricket, one laden with disappointments as well as trophies, I have always remembered those snapshots of another life, and realise how fortunate I have been to make a living as a sportsman. It might seem surprising to those members and spectators who saw me as a gnarled old pro totally immersed in the game, but before a cup final at Lord's I would stress to my Essex players that defeat would not be a disaster. We wanted to win as much as any other team, but I tried to impart to them that this was of scant importance compared to living in penury or a life ebbing away in a hospice. I like to think this relaxed them and was a factor in the success we had. I would not have enjoyed playing under, say, Geoffrey Boycott because the atmosphere in the dressing room and on the pitch would have been altogether too serious. Win or lose, Essex retained a sense of enjoyment and of humour. I endeavoured to do so as well.

So when I was sacked by England as both captain and coach, I was able to keep a sense of perspective by contemplating the alternatives in east London. I might conceivably have worked with my brother, who spent forty years as a pig farmer. He enjoyed and made a great success of his work, but I am not sure I would have relished it. I remain fortunate that I possessed some sporting ability.

Nowadays, I don't know anybody in the game who has to find a job outside it. In the autumn of 1968, when I signed on the dole after the tour of South Africa had been called off so late, I had to go before a tribunal and emphasise the seasonal nature of my work, before being paid any benefits. The fact that I won the case was subsequently of considerable importance to unemployed cricketers. At least the publicity this engendered led to subsequent winter employment from an oil company, which I gratefully took up.

I look back now in contentment. If I had been a more selfish person, I would have scored more Test runs or even accepted an invitation to captain the first breakaway tour to South

Africa in 1982 when my captaincy of England was not assured. Trevor Bailey, for one, my old Essex captain, thought I should have been more ruthless, but I am not at all sure that would have brought me more fulfilment. It might, I suppose, have meant I was more assured of my place. The early 1970s was a period I particularly enjoyed because I was batting well, but I simply did not have it in me to put myself ahead of the team. I am all too aware that if I had coached England at a different time – preferably now – I would have remained in the job for longer and maybe been in the happy position of reckoning, as I never did at the time, that we had a team good enough to beat Australia.

If I were a young batsman now, I would possibly be a contracted player and this would give me more peace of mind as well as far better remuneration. A cricketer good enough to play for England this week is good enough to do so next week as well. I always felt under pressure to score runs and hence I never really relaxed when playing Test cricket. I knew that if I didn't bat well enough for two consecutive Tests, I'd be dropped, even when I appeared to have a settled place in the early 1970s. This was in part because a higher standard of county cricket meant a greater number of good batsmen could be called upon, but also because the prevailing thinking dictated that a team could be changed frequently.

A central contract today would have meant I'd have played Test cricket more frequently and would probably have taken part in 180 one-day internationals, and benefited accordingly from the finance that Sky, in particular, has injected. It is hard to convey now the prevalent feeling in the 1960s and 1970s that cricketers should play for the love of the game. Indeed they should, but bills still have to be paid. This was, I think, a hangover from the days when amateur ideals held sway, but foresight was decidedly lacking. Before World Series Cricket, the crowds were big enough to attract enough revenue to pay the players more than trifling sums. Nobody in a position of authority appeared to feel this would be a just thing to do, or considered that a predatory figure such as Kerry Packer might be attracted to the game – a businessman who through his sheer wealth was able to lure even the great Garry Sobers and Richie Benaud to his cause, which provided him with the necessary cloak of respectability.

As a batsman, the most trying period of my career was when I was on the horrendous tour of Australia in 1974–75. I made a sequence of low scores and was subsequently left out and labelled as someone who couldn't play the pace of Dennis Lillee and Jeff Thomson. I have long disliked this kind of simplistic thinking because a bowler as competent as Lillee and one as quick as Thomson would have dismissed anyone in any era of the game. Dennis Amiss, a very fine opener, was also in and out of the team. In the 1970s, Marcus Trescothick would not have remained at the top of the order without making runs, but now Duncan Fletcher, one of my successors, is allowed to back his own judgement. He has his own pool of centrally contracted players and sticks to it. Hence Trescothick, when he is short of runs, is granted the time and opportunities to play himself back into form.

Timing and luck, good or ill, accounts for a great deal in cricket. I was as aware of this when having to face Lillee, perhaps the finest bowler in the game's history, as I was when I became coach. In the 1990s, we fielded some of the weakest teams in the history of English cricket but there is no purpose served in fretting over that. To gain the friendship and respect of my peers was, I believe, of greater importance than scoring more runs and obtaining an improved batting average, and this I hope I achieved. One reason for this is that I have never been a slave to averages and cannot remember what mine was without looking it up in *Wisden*. In my fifth decade in the game, I can think of only a couple of individuals, both Yorkshiremen who were rather obsessed about their own facts and figures, whom I would not care to invite into my home. Many of my colleagues, particularly at county level, have been lifelong friends.

One of the reasons why I look back on my time with Essex with more fondness than I do on international cricket is because the Test teams had no sense of unity. No established players ever gave me advice on batting or what certain bowlers were likely to do with the ball. Even when we won the Ashes in Australia in 1970–71, which would have been *the* highlight of most cricketers' careers, we were just a bunch of individuals coming together under the banner of MCC, some of whom looked after themselves and did not bother to assist newcomers. None of the comradeship that was found among county players, who were with one another all the time, was in evidence. We won because we were better than the opposition. There were happier tours, particularly under Tony Lewis to India and Pakistan in 1972–73, but the introduction of central contracts has resulted in England effectively becoming, in terms of spirit and cohesion, a county team.

When I was an international player, I just went out and did my job. Playing cricket was something I loved doing but it *was* a job, and one that entailed spending long periods away from home. I wasn't around for the birth of either of my children. My first daughter, Tara, arrived during a Test match I was playing in at Leeds, and my second daughter, Sarah, during a tour, so I didn't see her until she was three months old. I don't think I'd have been allowed to return home and if I had, I'd have had to pay the air fare and I couldn't afford it. Michael Vaughan would never have been permitted to interrupt a Test to see his daughter born had he played twenty or thirty years ago.

So much has altered. Unlike Vaughan, I suspect, I wouldn't know how to change a nappy. When I was left in charge of my daughters for a day, I took them down to a friend's house. It was the way things were. I missed a great deal of their upbringing but I had to earn a living and in my playing days, wives were rarely allowed to come on tour. Not until 1974–75, six years after I made my Test debut, did this change and then our heavy defeat by Australia gave rise to criticism that the wives and children were distracting influences, which was nonsense. By then, I was thinking seriously about whether I wanted to be away for that length of time without having my family present for at least some of the tour. In India and Pakistan in 1972–73 I was away for nearly six months without seeing them, although most of the hotels on that tour would not have been suitable, anyway. I am thankful that my marriage to Sue has been a strong one, and that Sarah and Tara have been understanding about an international sportsman's lot, so I don't feel my relationships with them have been affected. They accepted my job for what it was and mixed happily with the wives and children of the other Essex players while I was away.

I have not always relished the recognition that comes with being an international sportsman. I had to give up playing football, a game I enjoyed, when some over-zealous opponents tried to chop me down. This was at village level and my sole offence, so far as I could make out, was to be an England cricketer. Pubs or bars always seemed to include some objectionable individuals, especially in Australia. Each year when

I was in the limelight I would receive cranky letters and once, when I was England coach, I received a parcel that looked suspiciously like a home-made bomb.

In 1970, someone threatened to kill me on the grounds that I was working as a gamekeeper in my free time that winter. I had grown up in the country and, to me, shooting was just another sport. To this day I take a gun out or join a beat whenever I am invited. The police took the threat seriously and, as I had been married for only a short time, so did Sue. The letter writer, whose identity was never discovered, threatened to shoot me when I next stepped out of my home in Stebbing. Fortunately, nothing came of it.

I continued to receive hostile letters from people who were opposed to blood sports and I imagine these would have intensified in recent years if I had taken part in fox hunting. Foxes come into our village all the time and my response is that rural foxes may well become virtually extinct now that hunting has been banned. Farmers will simply cull them in the same way that they are forced to cull deer intermittently on account of sheer numbers. It is easily forgotten that man has hunted, shot and fished –too popular a sport to be a target for politicians – since the days of the cavemen.

The vilification I received when I was coach – or manager, as I was optimistically styled – of a weak England team ranged from critical faxes sent to our hotel in Australia to a demand to recall David Gower when I was having a drink in an extremely quiet bar on the Algarve one autumn. Even ex-pats wanted to have their say. The simplest way to avoid any trouble was to get up and leave. I have never thought of myself as an obtrusive or especially opinionated person, but even now, when I visit some far-flung county ground to assess a particular player, I am swiftly recognised. I find that my deerstalker and coat are no disguise. I like to talk to the genuine enthusiast and do not deliberately stay away from the pavilion, but I can do without the scarcely veiled hostility of others.

Recognition, of course, was inevitable once I became England captain in 1981. There was no greater honour than that appointment. My father, who had always been supportive since we played together in the same village team, appreciated it as much as I did. My mother, alas, had died earlier that year. Of course, I realised I was no more than a stopgap. Others, notably Ian Botham, had had a go and his successor, Mike Brearley, was not continuing only because he did not wish to tour any more. I was 37 by then and thought I would probably lead the team that winter against India and the following summer against India and Pakistan. As it was, we had a frustrating and dull series on the sub-continent, were defeated 1–0 – although that was hardly a calamity – and I was stripped of the captaincy by my boyhood hero, Peter May, partly, I feel, so that a younger batsman could have my middle-order place. Again, no spirit of togetherness pervaded the team, not least because the first breakaway tour to South Africa was hatched during the winter, although I hold no resentment towards the players for planning that without informing me until after we had arrived back from India. I was never to meet May again, which I regret. I would have liked to discover his reasoning.

The importance of equilibrium was never more necessary than on the 1994 Caribbean tour when we were bowled out for 46 by the West Indies in Trinidad. This was during my two and a half years as England coach and that result confirmed for me how much more difficult and less rewarding the role was compared to playing. I was not in control of our destiny. I was too dependent on the quality, or lack of it, in the team.

Nasser Hussain reckoned my position was doomed after that, and yet I had not been able to go to the wicket myself to try to do something about it. I always enjoyed being in the middle more than coaching from the pavilion. My relationship with the players was totally different and more distanced, partly because of my role, partly on account of my age. On most of evenings of that tour I ate with the tour manager, Bob Bennett or M.J.K. Smith, and the scorer. There were, of course, high spots, such as when Alec Stewart scored two centuries in the Test in Barbados and we won the match, but leading Essex to all four titles in England, becoming the only captain to achieve that in domestic cricket, ultimately meant more to me.

None of this should suggest that I have followed an unhappy career path. My memories are mostly of pleasant people and of the joy of being paid for pursuing the prime interest in my life. The sense of team spirit and companionship I encouraged, which was to benefit Essex to such an extent in the 1970s and 1980s, was forged in my own life at home. My father, a sheet-metal worker who ran a men's drinking club in the evening to make ends meet, played village cricket in Cambridgeshire. He was not good enough to play at a higher level and did not aspire to be. Matches would start at 2.30 and we would not be home before midnight, when the bar closed.

I am not sure from which member of the family I inherited my sporting ability. I had a close relationship with my parents and inherited my father's ability to get on with all sorts of different people. It meant that, on tour, I was put down to share a room with the more awkward members of the party, ranging from Basil D'Oliveira, who would trash furniture after too much to drink, to Derek Randall, who would wake me at 3 a.m. to ask whether I would like a cup of tea. I endeavoured to get on with them all, which made touring tolerable.

I learned the value of mixing well at a young age. Even though I possessed no proper kit, I was a regular member of our village team in Cambridgeshire, Caldecote, by the age of 11. We played on a ground that was no more than a cowfield – literally. After school on Fridays I had to assist with cleaning up the dung that lay all over the square. Then the pitch had to be cut and rolled. Only once all that had been done could anybody start any net practice. The tolerance and encouragement I received from the grown-ups around me was, I am sure, a factor in making me appreciate the necessity for team spirit and unity. That was not evident when I started to play for Essex, for there were still clear lines of seniority. When I became captain in 1974 and later, when I led England, I was determined that the younger cricketers would not be overawed or silenced.

My development as a batsman was simply, I believe, on account of having an eye for a ball. Trevor Bailey said that if I had grown up in America, I would have become a tennis or baseball player. I never had the opportunity to play tennis as a boy but football, as I've said, and hockey both appealed to me. I played hockey for Cambridgeshire but cricket was the priority, in spite of the village pitches and not being properly coached until I joined Essex. For Caldecote, I started off down the order but was soon promoted to open the batting with my father. By the time I was 13 I was playing for Royston, the nearest sizeable club to my home and, indeed, Jack Hobbs's old club, and trying to hone my technique by standing in front of a mirror for hours on end while studying *The Art of Cricket* by Sir Donald Bradman. I spent just as many hours sharpening my reactions by hitting a rubber ball attached to a piece of elastic. Years later

I met Sir Donald in Australia and was able to tell him what I had learned, which pleased him. He would come into the dressing room and had no compunction about helping any England cricketer, even when we were playing against Australia.

For much of my youth and in the initial stages of my career as a first-class cricketer, I played on poor pitches. I think it is fair to say that had I learned the game on better squares at The Oval or Lord's instead of on the indifferent out-grounds Essex played on before Chelmsford became our headquarters, I would have been a more prolific batsman. Groundsmen could produce squares more or less as they liked in those days without fear of incurring a penalty, and gravitating to a decent pitch after being accustomed to batting on a poor one was not as easy as it may sound. Bailey and Gordon Barker, the captain and senior professional, did not try to curtail my naturally attacking game. They reasoned that if I could hit a good ball to the boundary in indifferent conditions, I should be allowed to continue to do so.

Nowadays, a young cricketer's potential is identified much more quickly and thoroughly. The coaching structure is such that county clubs spend a great deal of money putting boys through their junior teams and academies and, understandably, are miffed if no loyalty is shown to them in return. Essex and, indeed, England in the 1960s, were unprofessional teams. There was no limbering up or fielding practice and players had to find alternative employment in the winter months. Some – not just me – were forced to go on the dole. The imponderable question is to what extent the fitness regimes and diets of today would have benefited the cricketers of those days, the best ones in particular. Would cutting out alcohol and running around the ground have made Tom Graveney, my first England captain, a finer batsman?

Has the game changed for the better? In some respects, yes, in some, no. I bemoan the absence of characters, the fact that bleep (fitness) tests, bland pitches without bite and turn, and bio-mechanics have taken some of the soul out of the game. There are too many robotic cricketers who do not talk enough about the game or learn from their opponents in the bar afterwards because a series of dour coaches tell them not to fraternise and to go away and do their warm-downs instead. Once, in the 1970s, when Keith Pont was directed to field at third man at the start of an over from the same position at the other end of the ground, he borrowed a spectator's bicycle and cycled around the boundary. That zest for life and the game lifted the rest of my Essex team and ensured any monotonous repetition would be punctuated with good humour. It was instrumental in the wonderful success we had but such behaviour would be frowned upon now.

As I go around the country in my present, and final, role with Essex – I do not care for serving on committees – assessing the merits of young players and the strength of opponents, occasionally I am lucky enough to come across a batsman such as Alastair Cook, who is just about the best young cricketer I have ever seen. I see talent, enthusiasm and, quite often, application but I also observe too much appealing, especially from the boundary edge, unattractive sledging in club cricket and a game that, in spite of England's successes under another, unrelated, Fletcher, is still suffocated by the attention given to football. One day that may change – but I suspect not in my lifetime. I regret the lack of festival cricket, uncovered pitches and, especially, spin bowling. Ashley Giles deserves much credit for having made all he could of his ability but he would not have progressed beyond county cricket when I started in the game. The craftsman has to be nurtured more than the handyman.

I intensely dislike the reliance by many a county on expedience – the overseas performers who stay for six weeks at a cost of £35,000 or £40,000 each. No wonder Sport England are threatening to withdraw subsidy to the game on the basis that too much money is going to overseas players. What are Kent, the county who developed the best home-grown cricketers of my playing days, thinking of in allowing Ed Smith and Alex Loudon to leave, even though they wanted to go elsewhere, and signing a string of discarded players from other counties and four overseas cricketers in one season? Why were Middlesex fielding Sven Koenig, an opening batsman in his thirties who has never come close to playing Test cricket for South Africa and who was inevitably drawn to London by the strength of the pound against the rand, ahead of Denis Compton's grandson, Nick? The salaries paid to average county cricketers are far too high. No wonder the England and Wales Cricket Board (ECB) has to procure as much money as it can from Sky to prop up the domestic game.

Offset against such myopia are the benefits of the modern game, not merely in the form of central contracts but also the new Academy at Loughborough and the support given to the England coach where none existed before. The arrival of specialist coaches is to be applauded, not least Troy Cooley, who has made such a difference to the fast bowlers, as is the greater consistency in the selection and retention of a player at Test level until his worth is proven one way or the other. Above all, the unearthing of exciting talent must be encouraged. Andrew Flintoff is providing the dash and verve that English cricket has lacked for too long. Boys need heroes and here, through dint of perseverance – for initially he was not impressive – is someone who not only plays like one but looks like one, too.

I still maintain that central contracts would not have been necessary had the first-class counties cooperated fully with the requirements of the England coach, but there is no doubting their introduction has made an immense difference, not just in terms of results but in the significance attached to playing for England. Test cricketers are well remunerated, which makes a career in the game that much more attractive for a young person, unless he is drawn towards football. Top players can afford to buy expensive houses, which would have been unthinkable for an England captain out of his earnings in the past. Peter May and Ted Dexter retired early in part because they needed to earn more money than they could do playing cricket in the 1960s, even though the era of the unpaid amateur was at an end. Whisper it quietly, but cricketers of today have much to be grateful to Kerry Packer for. He improved their lot with his World Series Cricket, even if he did nothing for the pleasantries of the game. Players of my generation had to rely on the benefit seasons they were awarded after ten years as first-team cricketers. The money raised was supposed to be enough to buy a four-bedroomed house, although the sums accrued varied considerably from county to county. You were unlikely to fare so well in Derbyshire as you were in Surrey. The system did have the distinct advantage of rewarding loyalty, a trait that has gone out of fashion in cricket, as it has within the wider community, due not least to the advent of two divisions in the County Championship. As in football, the best players today want to play for the best clubs.

Other than my family, the game has given me everything I possess – friendships, a lovely house as a result of a benefit season and a testimonial year, and international recognition, encompassing travel far and wide. To have captained Essex and England was to reach a pinnacle. The setbacks linger in the mind but I do not bear grudges because the game has meant too much to me. The enthusiasm I possessed as a boy when I undertook an eight-hour return trip from my home in Cambridgeshire, lugging my bat and bag to the rickety old cricket school at Ilford, has never left me. I used to catch the 7.30 bus to Cambridge, the 9.30 train to Liverpool Street, the underground to Gants Hill and then walk a mile to Beehive Lane indoor cricket school, now owned by Nasser Hussain's father, carrying my kit. I thought nothing of it but in an age in which everybody seems to travel everywhere by car, no youngster will want to hear what it was like in my day. I would only be told I am starting to sound like dear old Alec Bedser.

CHAPTER 1

ASHES TO ASHES

I started and ended my career in Test cricket against Australia and neither occasion was an enjoyable experience. In 1968, when I had no real notion of what the international game was like, and no manager or senior player dispensed advice, I was out for a duck. Twenty-six years later, when I was struggling to make the most of individuals who simply were not good enough, we lost the Ashes and I lost my job as England coach. In between, other series and matches are no less seared in the memory. We triumphed on my first England tour, in 1970–71, when Ray Illingworth, a constant in my time in the game, excelled in his tactics and leadership. We were beaten four years later on uneven pitches against one of the most hostile pair of fast bowlers in the history of the game, Dennis Lillee and Jeff Thomson. In 1977 I played in the Centenary Test in Melbourne, which was one of the most charged matches I ever took part in. When I was a player, neither country was in the ascendancy for longer than a series or two. By the time I became coach, the matches were worryingly one-sided. The Ashes, the symbol of cricketing excellence, were devalued.

One of my daughters visited Australia recently and took to the people she encountered. I could never do that and one day I shall return to the country and explore it properly to see what I've missed. My tour itineraries comprised hotels, grounds, receptions – and ear-bashings. There was little social-ising between the sides. In England, the tradition was to repair to the bar at close of play, and as a county captain, I was given an allowance for entertaining. I learned from discussing the day's play with my opposite number, the umpires and senior pros. However, Australia in the 1970s did not go in for pubs or places to drink inside Test stadiums. Instead, their players liked to bring a crate of beer into the visitors' dressing room, but this was not encouraged by Illingworth or Ian Chappell or, in later years when emphasis was placed on warm-downs, by the coaches. Besides, I could not bring myself to open a bottle and take part in banter with chippy, chirpy people who had just been trying to knock my head off.

The only Australian cricketers I came to know were those who played for Essex. Allan Border, who made his runs when we needed them on a green top or when the ball was lifting, and the languidly elegant Mark Waugh were high-class players and I liked them both. Border was aggressive and led by the way he played. I believe he learned a lot playing under me – indeed he said so in his book. I stressed the importance of thinking about winning from the first ball of the match, which Border took on board and turned to Australia's advantage when he captained them in England in 1989. He had become a bit too friendly with the opposition on their previous tour of England in 1985, when they were defeated, and I did not believe in that. We could have a laugh and a joke on the field but we played our cricket in a hard way. Merv Hughes, who as a youngster was in the Essex second XI, lived up to his image. He and Alan Lilley once stripped Neil Burns, our young wicket-keeper, and staked him down, naked, in the middle of the pitch at Chelmsford during net practice. Bruce Francis, one of our first overseas signings, was the one Australian I came across who played the game more like a club cricketer than a pro. These were good team-mates who gave their all.

From a distance, one or two other Aussies, such as Doug Walters, appeared likeable, but some others, including Ian Chappell, I found aggressive and unpleasant and they seemed not to want to attend the receptions we were all obliged to attend. The spectators and the Australians we met at receptions and restaurants were always telling us how useless we were and how we were going to be thrashed. They became even more outspoken after a few beers and we just had to accept it as part of a tour to Australia. Not all Aussies are like that, I'm sure – I must take my daughter's word for it.

The prime advantage that Australia has always had over northern hemisphere countries is, of course, the climate. In an outdoor society, boys want to bowl. They are not concerned about pulling muscles or slippery run-ups. They would not be so keen to run in or undertake fielding practice on a freezing spring day at Cambridge, where there is no protection from the winds whipping across the Fens and no hiding from a stinging ball on fingers that should still be wrapped in mittens.

The different outlooks in England and Australia will not change. In England, we think about socialising at tea and after the match, and going down to the pub or clubhouse in the evening. In Australia, they think about winning and then going home. There is no village cricket in Australia and club cricket, the route into state and Test sides, is taken really seriously. Even Australian international players take part in grade matches and players such as the Waughs, Steve and Mark, are still associated with the clubs they first played for, whereas potential England cricketers progress through age groups at county level in a more sheltered way. In Australia, boys play against men much earlier than in England.

Take the Essex premier league, which has two divisions and a system of promotion and relegation. I find that players don't want to travel to a ground for an 11.30 start on a Saturday with fielding practice beforehand. As for not being able to field two sides for 2 p.m. starts and giving coaching expenses to large number of overseas players who are not permitted to be paid at this level, it would never happen in Australia, where they play such matches over two weekends. We do not have a hope of introducing a system similar to the Australians' and the powers that be realise that now. In club cricket in Sydney, there are no more than ten overseas players. In Essex as elsewhere, we send players to Paul Terry's Academy in Perth to toughen them up. They think on their feet more, do not have an attendant to bring them refreshments and come back better and more rounded cricketers, even though the coaching is not any improvement on what they have hitherto been accustomed to. Yet back in 1970–71, I felt English county cricket to be of a higher standard than Australian state cricket.

My initial experience of playing against Australia was at Headingley in 1968. What should have been an occasion to remember turned out to be the most unpleasant time of my career. From a young age I had been marked out as a future Test cricketer by Trevor Bailey, so expectations hung over me. I was selected, having been twelfth man for the previous Test at Edgbaston, because Colin Cowdrey was injured, and I soon discovered that even such established batsmen as

Cowdrey and Kenny Barrington would not pass on their knowledge or give tips on how to combat a particular bowler and it would have been considered a weakness on my part to have asked them. Tom Graveney would dispense advice if asked but the prevailing attitude was one of each to his own. Even players of this ability were afraid of losing their places to up-and-coming batsmen.

Geoffrey Boycott looked after himself and I was wary of John Edrich. Basil D'Oliveira, whom I liked, had come into English cricket ten years later than he should have done and did not have any particular friend in the England dressing room. When I got to know him, he would talk about his past from time to time and say how lucky he was to have been encouraged by John Arlott and Graveney. I admired him and the way he batted, using his strong forearms to play spinners off the back foot. Once, when he returned from some late-night drinking session, he made such a noise that Boycott, across the way, came to complain. D'Oliveira could not stand him, so it was fortunate Boycott scampered back to his room and put the chain on the door while I restrained my room-mate.

So my abiding memories of my debut are less to do with Australians than the attitude of the England players and the Yorkshire spectators, who made it quite plain that they wanted Phil Sharpe to play ahead of me. He had been a late addition to the customary twelve players, selected to cover for a batsman who might not have been able to play owing to injury. The spectators who came on that first morning did not appreciate – or did not want to appreciate – that Sharpe was not only unlikely to be included but would not be chosen ahead of me. My only problem was that he, like Cowdrey, was a specialist first slip and, in the absence of anybody else thought capable of fielding there, this was where I was positioned by Graveney.

It was not a position I liked, although Graveney would not have known that. I had fielded there for Essex when spinners were deployed. Throughout my career there was a dearth of natural first slips and even John Snow found himself directed to go there at times. Graveney's preference was for third or fourth slip, where he could watch the ball off the bat rather than from the bowler's hand. It sounds an insignificant matter, but the two positions really are very different and appeal to diverse individuals. Sharpe, like Cowdrey and Peter Parfitt, was a specialist who never fielded anywhere else, except in one-day cricket.

The upshot was that I dropped two chances off Snow on the first morning and was jeered by the crowd for the rest of the match. One chance was to my left, the other to my right, and both were difficult, but naturally I felt despondent. Various hecklers made it quite clear that they thought Sharpe should have been fielding there in my place. Worse followed. The most important thing for me was to make runs in my first Test match to alleviate the pressure, but it didn't happen. England were 209 for four when I went in. I faced a couple of overs without undue concern until, shaping to glance the medium-paced Alan Connolly away to leg, I was adjudged caught behind by Barry Jarman. The ball, I am certain, flicked only my thigh pad, but I was given out by umpire Syd Buller and those spectators who had wanted to see Sharpe play instead of me mocked me as I returned to the pavilion. I could not comprehend the attitude of supposed cricket lovers, given that this was a Test match against Australia. At least in the second innings of what was a drawn match I did make some runs – an unbeaten 23 – following some bizarre advice from Graveney. 'Play for a draw, but make it look good,' he said. I was dropped after that match, Cowdrey having recovered from injury.

From then on, I was never assured of an England place, not least because throughout my career any number of good middle-order batsmen were available. One of many improved aspects of Test cricket now is that a young cricketer is given more than one match to prove himself. I was not to face Australia again until the next tour there, two winters later. Self-doubt persisted even after I had made my first Test century, against New Zealand in 1973. I never went through a particularly bad patch of form but there was no one I could telephone for advice or ask for an assessment of what I was doing wrong. If asked, Trevor Bailey would pass on his thoughts when he was summarising for Test Match Special – he reckoned I should have made more runs – but he did not like to come into the dressing room and, as a member of the media, would have been excluded anyway. I think he felt it was no longer his place to dispense advice.

Touring was not a particularly attractive proposition then. The days when MCC parties set forth by ship and were feted, wined and dined wherever they went had gone by the early 1960s. In 1968 I was chosen for the aborted tour of South Africa, a venue everyone would have relished unashamedly for no other reasons than style and comfort. Instead, we were re-routed to a yet more troublesome part of the world, Pakistan. It was one matter following the sun but quite another to be playing in the dry heat of the sub-continent. This was before anyone routinely wore sunglasses and our eyes were burned by the glare off the pitches. The tour lasted six weeks but it felt like six long months. The country was virtually in a state of civil war, the cricket was dull and the facilities generally poor. Student law prevailed in some places and we needed the protection of armed guards wherever we journeyed. The tour should never have taken place.

From a personal perspective, I made some runs – 83 in four hours in the drawn First Test – but this was of scant significance considering that the tour ended in chaos with the abandonment of the Third Test at Karachi. We had to flee the country without alerting the student mob, who undoubtedly would have turned against us and obstructed our departure. The sight of the riot police taking on a crowd running across the pitch was the nearest I have come to being directly involved in hooliganism at a sports ground. I dreaded my next visit there.

If selected, I went on whatever tour England had organised simply because I had no alternative; I had to earn some money. I married at a young age and to be separated from my family was quite dreadful. For many years wives were not welcomed on these trips – 'a cricket tour is no more a place for them than the Somme', as John Woodcock wrote in *The Times* – and when Sue came to Australia in 1970–71, the cost of her flight and her expenses meant that, although she managed to see a new country, I earned precisely nothing that winter. Such visits are subsidised these days.

Playing for England was not well rewarded in those pre-Packer days – the fee was around £100 a Test – but at least I knew I could make a living from the game. I was never dropped by Essex or feared being injured. If my game was affected, it was not so much through financial worries – I was completely focused on having to make runs – but through Essex having a poor side when I started. This meant I had to be more defensive in outlook than I might otherwise have been because the whole side could easily have crumbled. I was fortunate to receive a benefit and a testimonial. It was far harder for Graham Saville and Alan Lilley, who were struggling on the fringe of the Essex side. When I became captain

I did my utmost to look after them and tried to ensure they were awarded benefits, although Saville, a first-team player for only two years, never did receive one. The old maxim of treating people nicely on the way up in the expectation that they will reciprocate is an apt one.

The two series I played in Australia were effectively decided by pace bowling, and, on the first of them, the batting of Geoffrey Boycott. In 1970–71 John Snow was at his peak, obtaining pace and movement off the seam and troubling all the upper order batsmen. The Australians had the utmost respect for him throughout his career and it is no coincidence that we lost in 1974–75 when neither he nor Geoff Boycott were on the tour. The other, highly significant reason for our defeat on that tour was the recovery of Lillee from injury and the emergence of Thomson, whose unusual slinging action made sighting the ball that much harder. What was swiftly apparent was that the pair of them did not want for the devil that is a necessary part of a fast bowler's make-up.

I had played against Lillee when he first appeared in Test cricket on the 1970–71 tour. Although he was young and erratic, he quite clearly possessed the single most important attribute for a potential fast bowler – pace. That was equally evident on his successful tour of England in 1972, although he was beginning to suffer from a stress fracture of the back that afflicted him further in the Caribbean. He was not expected to recover in time for our visit in 1974–75, if at all, and the initial reports we read or received were that he was coming in at a gentle medium in state matches for Western Australia. As for Thomson, he initially seemed more of a beach bum than a cricketer and had played in just one Test

match, against Pakistan, without any joy. We did not anticipate that he would have much of a role in the series.

We did not anticipate the uneven pitch of mottled grass
and variable bounce for the First Test at Brisbane, either. It
was cut by a groundsman who, curiously, doubled as the local
mayor. For Sydney, the venue for the Fourth Test, a great
deal of grass was deliberately left on the pitch. It made no
difference that Alec Bedser, our tour manager, complained
about poor preparation. Buoyed by such encouraging conditions, Lillee swiftly demonstrated that he had regained his
speed, bowling within himself for six balls of an eight-ball
over and then sending down a couple of quick balls without
any discernible change in his action. He had everything – he
swung the ball out, he was aggressive, his run-up was rhythmical and he kept running in. It made no difference to him
if the temperature was 104 degrees in the shade.

Lillee was the best bowler I ever faced, although Fred
Trueman, whom I faced as a teenager in 1963, was exceptional, too. Thomson was the quicker at the start of the tour,
at around 92mph, but once Lillee had fully recovered from
his back trouble, which he had by the end of the series, he
was quicker still. However, once the ball arrives at over 90mph,
it is hard to discern any difference. What with the West Indian
fast bowlers as well, more individuals of extreme pace were
plying their trade in this era than at any other time. This
embarrassment of bowling riches eventually spawned helmets,
arm guards and inner-thigh protectors, none of which I felt
comfortable wearing. Nor did I like my vision to be obscured
by any form of grill and only utilised this at the end of my
career, when I did not trust my reactions.

In retrospect, I should have tried to play differently on that
1974–75 tour of Australia. I would have been better off making

my initial trigger movement forward rather than backwards, in spite of the disconcerting state of the pitches and my natural concern about facing excessive pace and short-pitched bowling. Many of the best players in the modern era, not least the leading pullers and cutters, aim to move on to the front foot and attack the ball – much more so than in the past. Viv Richards – until he was older and seeking to protect his wicket more than when he was in his prime – Gordon Greenidge, Ricky Ponting and Matthew Hayden are notable examples. Australia's upper order is adept at this. In the mid 1970s, too much emphasis was placed on trying to grind the bowling down and on experimentation with forward and backward movement, not least from Cowdrey. There was no coach accompanying the touring party.

I never managed to master the art of leaving the short ball that was going to pitch on or outside off stump and rise harmlessly above it on the hard, Australian surfaces. Bobby Simpson and Ian Redpath perfected this but my grounding in very different conditions meant that I did not have the confidence to leave it unless the ball was obviously going well wide of the stumps. Australian batsmen would never attempt this when playing in England, but they seemed to be able to adjust their approach accordingly. Tony Greig and Alan Knott resolved that the best way to counter the steepling bounce was to upper cut Lillee and Thomson over the slips to third man. Typically competitive, Greig did not stop there. He would signal a boundary to rile Lillee, who would lose his rag and his direction. Greig reasoned that the pace of the ball was such that, even if he edged it, the shot would fly over the slips, and if he wound up the bowlers, who were giving us so few balls to score off, they would not bowl so well. Instead of following his example and trying to score runs off the rest of the attack, we tried to battle it out. The back-up bowlers were Max Walker, who was no more than a good county medium pacer, and Ashley Mallet, who was suited to bowling off-spin on hard pitches. He made the ball drop rather than drift away from the bat but he would have been slogged in England.

In Sydney, when Greig was bowling at him, Lillee was struck on the elbow – unfortunately his left one, so his ability to bowl was unimpaired. I picked up his bat to hand it back to him and said to Greig something along the lines of, 'Let him have it.' We had had enough of the constant short-pitched bowling and not having anyone who could frighten the Australians in return. Peter Lever, Chris Old and Geoff Arnold were not nearly so quick, and nor, at that stage of his career, was Bob Willis.

Lillee responded with a stream of abuse, inevitably, given his piratical nature, so I threw his bat on the ground and let him pick it up himself. That night, on television, he vowed revenge and when I came in to bat the next day, the crowd was not so much expectant as frenzied, seemingly regarding this as theatre, if not war. 'Kill! Kill!' were the accompanying cries as I made my way to the wicket and I was ducking almost before the ball left Lillee's hand. My comment to Greig and gesture of throwing away the bat may have seemed pointless and ill-advised, but the reality was that nothing we did or said would have made any difference. It seems extraordinary now that no player or manufacturer came up with a prototype for a helmet during that series and indeed did not do so for another couple of years, when Sunil Gavaskar and Mike Brearley started wearing a kind of skull cap. Several times that winter I saw balls so late that they missed my face only by inches and, on one horrendous occasion, one from Lillee reared from short of a length between Geoff Arnold's nose and flailing bat, cleared Rodney Marsh standing well back and thudded into the sightscreen. That unnerved even the bowler.

Although I never wanted to mix socially with the Australians in the way that Greig did at close of play, laughing and joking about his antics over a few beers in the dressing room, I met Lillee a few times at matches and receptions in later years and he was perfectly affable. The similarities between him and Ian Botham, not least their endless intentions to try to drink each other under the table, are marked, and I should imagine he, like Botham, would be extremely loyal to his friends. They enjoy the good life.

At the time, I found it too hard to detach myself from what was happening in the middle to want to fraternise during a Test match. I was peeved, too, that the umpires were weak and not respected by either Lillee or Ian Chappell, both of whom were rude to them. They should have had far more control over short-pitched bowling. This all went back to the 'bodyline' series of 1932–33 and got out of hand on the third-rate pitches. The only difference now was that there was a restriction on fielders behind the wicket on the leg side. Sir Donald Bradman spoke out about it and Alec Bedser had a quiet word with the Australian Cricket Board but nothing was done. If we had had Lillee and Thomson on our side, the Australian press would have savaged us as they did in 1970–71 when Snow hit Terry Jenner, a tailender, on the head, the upshot of him refusing to walk in a state match. It was the only bouncer Snow bowled at him so Illingworth could have been forgiven for getting in a rage with umpire Lou Rowan for reprimanding him. In fact, not that many bouncers were delivered in that series – approximately one every two overs. I remember in 1974–75 receiving four on the trot. An eight-ball over from Thommo would consist of four short-pitched ones, three that were so wide you couldn't reach them, and an outswinging 'jaffa'. Recognised batsmen who could duck could cope with this. Fred Titmus, Derek Underwood and Arnold could not pick up the short-pitched ball quickly enough.

How we missed Snow in that series. His omission was a dreadful selectorial blunder. At the very least, the batsmen would have benefited from better prepared pitches if the Australians had had to face him. He may have been past his best by then but he was still better than anybody else we had. He knew how to dismiss players such as Ian Chappell, Ian Redpath, Doug Walters and Rod Marsh and I bet they were delighted when they learned he was not coming. On tour, he would bowl at medium pace in the state matches; he needed the arena of Test cricket to give of his best. He would have been ideally suited to the present-day policy of central contracts. He would have loved that. As a fast bowler in Test cricket, he could be counted alongside the very best in the game – Lillee, Malcolm Marshall, Michael Holding, Andy Roberts and Allan Donald. At county level, you never quite knew what he was going to do, whether he would raise his game against you. Once, on the old Essex garrison ground at Colchester, he ran through us on a slow pitch after he had been left out of a Test. He had something to prove. Otherwise, unless it was a Gillette Cup match or he knew that the main cricket correspondents would be there, he could not motivate himself. Snow was a bit of a loner and certainly not the traditional beer-swilling quick bowler in the mould of Trueman, but a nice enough person.

I was never afraid of any fast bowler because I reckoned on being able to judge the length of the ball and I trusted my eyesight and reactions, but I was apprehensive in 1974–75. The hardest aspect of batting against fast bowling is when the surfaces are uneven. Lillee and Thomson were trying to hit us – although I did not for a moment believe any bombastic talk that they or any other fast bowlers wanted to cause injury – and even such excellent batsmen as Colin Cowdrey, who was summoned to cover for injuries, and Dennis Amiss were unnerved on that tour. Brian Luckhurst, a fine batsman at the start of the 1970s, never played again for England.

Thomson did strike me once on my MCC cap badge, but fortunately it didn't hurt. I still maintain that if only one of that opening pair had been playing for Australia, the series would have been very even; indeed, we might well have won. I finally ran into some form in the Fifth Test and carried it on to the Sixth, which was played at Melbourne on the best pitch of the series. Mike Denness and I both scored centuries, mine being my first in Australia. The difference now was that my confidence had returned and that both Thomson and Lillee, who began the match but broke down, were not fit. This was a notable triumph for Denness, the captain, who had left himself out of the Fourth Test on account of poor form, a decision I would not have taken had I been captain. I would have regarded it as a sign of weakness and would have resolved to fight my way out of a bad patch. Other than from John Inverarity, the batsman and schoolmaster who had a proper sense of perspective, I did not sense any especial sympathy or affection for Denness because of this gesture. The crowd showed no extra appreciation of his innings, or of England finally gaining a victory after the Ashes had been lost; not many Australians are good losers. They appreciate good cricket played against them – but only a certain amount.

The one person they did appreciate was Cowdrey, sent for

at short notice in time for the Second Test. This was his fifth tour of Australia over a period of twenty years and I have never observed more gutsy batting than when he took on Lillee and Thomson, whom he found a far harder proposition than Ray Lindwall and Keith Miller at the start of his Test career. He was almost 42 and had not played for England since 1971, although seemingly his Test career had come to an end as much through his disappointment over not captaining the 1970–71 party to Australia as any loss of form, for he continued to make runs in county cricket and would have merited a place on the 1974–75 tour from the outset.

I liked Cowdrey but did not find him an inspiring or strong leader. On my first tour, to Pakistan in 1969 when the crowds were rioting, it was quite evident he did not want to be there. For that matter, none of us did, but it was incumbent upon him to demonstrate more leadership and strength of purpose. I think he felt his life was in danger. Les Ames, the tour manager, who knew him better than anyone through their association at Kent, was left having to hold the party together. As a batsman, though, Cowdrey was of a high standing. He never butchered the ball. Whether at the crease or on his rare appearances on the golf course, where he still played off a handicap of around 8, or on the squash or real tennis court, he was a touch player. I have always believed that the best players of any era, be they from the 1930s or the 1990s, would have succeeded whenever they performed, and Cowdrey was no exception.

As with David Gower, it could be argued that Cowdrey's technique was not tight enough and that he lacked a steely edge. Had he been born a Yorkshireman with a love of all things pecuniary, I reckon he would have averaged five runs an innings more than he did. A need for money, which was not a concern of his, would have focused his mind more sharply. He was sufficiently well off not to have to rely on his performances to make a living.

Although a worrier off the field, he was completely relaxed on it, even when facing Lillee and Thomson. Having watched the First Test on television at home and having coped with Lindwall and Miller, Hall and Griffith and various other ogres, I suppose he reckoned they were just another fast-bowling pairing. I came to the conclusion that he was more at ease at the crease than anywhere else, although he was a fluent conversationalist and after-dinner speaker. I was also struck by how untidy he was. His kit would be strewn across the dressing-room, which was why I ended up with a pair of his cricket socks for years. I always reckoned that if I put six pairs into the communal wash, it did not bother me whose came out and into my possession. For some reason I never managed to return his and always wore them thereafter.

His two innings at Perth, on one of the quickest pitches in the world, after coming straight out of an English winter, realised scores of 22 and 40. These were reasonable scores in the context of the match and he did not flinch once from the endless bouncers. Years later, when I was England coach, we relived those events when Cowdrey invited me for shooting and dinner at his home near Arundel; I was amused that he did not have to concern himself with drink-driving as all the land around was owned by the Norfolk family, into which he had married. He could drive thirteen miles without going off the estate.

In 1974–75 it would have been instructive to have observed Boycott in opposition to Lillee and Thomson and, indeed, against the West Indian fast bowlers in England in 1976 when, I think, Tony Greig and the selectors were not keen to have him back. He had his reasons for not playing in either series but I do not believe there was any thought in his own mind of avoiding extreme pace. Boycott, it should not be forgotten, had to play against an equally ferocious attack in the Caribbean in 1980–81. He was, moreover, a gutsy player, and unfairly criticised for his slow batting. Without question he won more games for Yorkshire with the bat than anybody else since the war, which is to say since Len Hutton was in his prime. His technique was such that he could initially go forward and then move properly back – not many batsmen could cover the ball that started four inches outside off stump and nipped back.

I would criticise Boycott's approach to batting in one respect – and I make this point to young batsmen now. For 70 to 75 per cent of the time in which he was playing for himself he was also effectively playing for the team. The remaining 25 per cent of his batting should have been for the team and not for himself. It could be said that in the first innings of any match, a batsman should play for himself, whereas in the second innings he might have to go for quick runs. That's where Boycott was in the wrong. He was one-paced. The reason why he liked batting with Graham Gooch was that Gooch could take the pressure off him and hence he could play his own game. In contrast, a pairing of Boycott and Brian Luckhurst, both of whom toured Australia in 1970–71, was too one-dimensional. I made the mistake in India in 1981–82 of having Boycott and Chris Tavare positioned too close to each other in the batting order. The game never went anywhere when they were at the crease together and we played into India's hands as a result because they were 1-0 up at the time.

The reason, alas, why Boycott did not go to Australia in 1974–75 was because he was overlooked for the captaincy. He did not have enough respect for Mike Denness, who had captained him on the tour to the West Indies the previous winter. There might have been an element of pride in this or it could have been the result of feedback from other Kent and England players, such as Derek Underwood and Alan Knott, who rated Denness more highly as a captain in one-day cricket. It is hardly a novel observation to say that Boycott was self-centred. He would not help young batsmen in the England team, which probably came down to a fear of losing his place. To my mind, this was absolutely stupid. So, too, was his unwillingness to give of his knowledge when I captained him. Having said that, he was helpful later in assisting Gooch, Graham Thorpe and others when I was coaching England.

How would he have fared against Lillee and Thomson? At the very least, he would have been obdurate, although given how many balls wide of the stumps Thomson delivered, the rate of scoring would have been excruciatingly slow. He, incidentally, did not try wearing a helmet until 1979, after most of us had done so, which also gives the lie to any suggestion that he lacked courage against pace. By comparison, when the West Indies were thrashed by Australia a year after our visit, no one wanted to open the batting with Roy Fredericks or be padded up to go in as nightwatchman. There was no protective headgear and most certainly no respite against the quickest bowling.

Cowdrey had come to Australia well prepared with padded foam to protect his chest, but helmets did not become a standard part of the game until the gladiatorial contests of World Series Cricket began in 1977. I struggled to see through the visor, be it metal or plastic. The one time Gooch, one of the finest players of fast bowling, wore a visor was when he became concerned about opening an innings against the West Indian fast bowlers on an ill-prepared pitch in Kingston in 1986. We were fortunate, looking back to the 1960s and 1970s, that no one was killed, for in addition to batsmen wearing only caps and sun hats, short-leg fielders were at considerable risk. I was struck on the head once when fielding there, which left me in a dazed state, and on another occasion I was hit at silly point. I had to drop out of the following match because my head had swollen considerably.

In 1974–75 I recall John Edrich, who was a brave player of fast bowling, completely unruffled if he was beaten outside off stump, saying to me in the middle between overs, 'One tour too many, Fletch, one tour too many.' He was to make runs again on slower pitches in England but, in spite of my century in the final Test of the series – perhaps it was discounted because both fast bowlers were injured – I played just twice when the Australians returned for four Tests after the World Cup in the summer of 1975, and not at all when the West Indies followed in 1976. I seemed to be labelled as a batsman who had a weakness against fast bowling, which I refute. A bowler as good as Lillee will dismiss any batsman on his day when the conditions are in his favour – Hutton, Boycott, anyone. On other occasions, on flatter pitches, I reckoned to score runs off him or anybody else. The same went for Dennis Amiss during this period, and later, Michael Atherton when facing Glenn McGrath or Shaun Pollock. A technically adept player may lose confidence but he does not suddenly lose that expertise.

I am often asked about verbal aggression as practised by Lillee and McGrath. I do think our players were just as bad as the Aussies in terms of sledging during my first series there. Cowdrey, as England vice-captain, tried to distance himself from it, but by then there was no communication between him and Illingworth anyway and the fact that there were two camps – which I managed to straddle – made this a most difficult initial tour. I never took any notice of anything any Australian, or anybody else, said to me on the field of play – if someone had a go at me, I'd have a go back. Concentration has to be switched on and off at the crease by a batsman. That is part of the art of batting. It is not possible to remain at the crease for six hours otherwise. It helped, of course, that we had fast bowlers capable of making batsmen jump around, so that when Doug Walters came to the crease, the odd word of encouragement to Snow would not go amiss, for Walters did not play Snow well. I made a few comments myself but nothing derogatory. More recently, Atherton would have the odd chirp. What I don't care for when I watch young cricketers now is the mindless noise they make, particularly when they shout from the boundary edge. I have watched a great deal of Premier League cricket of late and seen players behave in a way that should have resulted in them being reprimanded. If someone goes over the top at any level, they should be dealt with. I doubt, for example, whether Merv Hughes would get away with quite so much now in this era of match referees, most certainly not if Clive Lloyd was in charge. Hughes got up people's noses. I didn't think he had the ability to take as many Test wickets as he did and believe he was obtaining an unfair edge through foul language rather than skill as a bowler.

As a result of not making enough runs against the Australians, I played intermittently for England in the 1970s. In 1971 I was selected for one Test, as was the case the following summer when Australia were back. Inevitably, I suppose, the match was at Headingley, my least favourite ground. I had just one innings and was out cheaply to the off-spin of Ashley Mallett.

It was about now that I was reaching my peak as a batsman and was regularly among the leading run-scorers in the country, and yet I had not achieved a score of note in a Test match in England. I can only surmise that the reason for this was that I was still not assured of a settled Test place.

That changed for a while in 1973. That summer was my most successful in the international game. I scored more runs in Test cricket than ever before, playing in all six Tests against, first, New Zealand and then the West Indies. My tally was 575 runs at an average in excess of 60. In the second Test against New Zealand at Lord's I made 178 in six and a quarter hours, my highest Test score at the time, and that innings prevented us from losing. The key to this lay in my being able to take runs off Vic Pollard, the off-spinner. The knowledge that I would retain my place gave me confidence and a sense of belonging. I batted consistently against the West Indies, a series that we lost on account of the brilliance of their batsmen and of their fast bowler Keith Boyce, my Essex colleague. My figures were starting to refute Illingworth's belief that I tended to bat better in the second innings of a Test than in the first. Boyce, a wonderfully athletic crowd-pleaser who could have become a superstar had he been English, and who became a good friend, seemed to save his fastest bowling for me. Yet I topped the averages in those three Tests, making 266 runs, and was made one of *Wisden*'s five cricketers of the year. Appropriately enough, the appreciation was written by Trevor Bailey. The three Essex boys he had picked out as being Test players of the future, Barry Knight, Graham Gooch and me, ultimately all made the grade.

The two tours that were sandwiched between England's visits to Australia in the early 1970s – to India and Pakistan and the West Indies – were, from a personal perspective, reasonably pleasing. We lost 2–1 in India in 1972–73 under the captaincy of the charming Tony Lewis, but competed really well. The selectors had declared publicly that this was to be 'my last chance' and I am glad to say that I performed better than any other batsman on the tour. After an indifferent start – I made 23 runs in my first four innings – I did well in the last three Tests. Tony Greig and I both achieved our maiden Test centuries at Bombay and I struck an unbeaten 97 on a turning pitch in Madras. Facing as talented a quartet of spinners as Chandrasekhar, Prasanna, Bedi and Venkataraghavan on turning pitches made for invigorating cricket. It was the reason why, leaving aside the state of some of the hotels in those days, India was my favourite country to tour. Prasanna buzzed through his off-spinners extremely well. Chandrasekhar bowled at the same pace as Derek Underwood and spun his leg-breaks appreciably. Bedi dropped the ball on to the seam with his lovely flight and loop.

None, though, could compare with Derek Underwood, who was more difficult to face than anybody. He was not so much a spinner of the ball, but more one who imposed cut on it. Contrary to the opinion of critics, including E.W. Swanton, who did not understand the game in the way that a pro did, Underwood would not have benefited from reducing his pace and attempting to turn the ball as Bedi did. I would have liked to face him if he had done, because he was not the kind of spinner who could bowl with similar flight and loop.

After India, we moved on to Pakistan for three Tests, all of which were drawn, in which I scored 221 runs. The British support for India over the Indo-Pakistani war resulted in open resentment towards us wherever we went. In Hyderabad we suffered from a sandstorm and in Karachi from more riots. In addition to this, the facilities in the guest houses we stayed in were poor. Overall, I never felt in any serious danger on my various trips to Pakistan and I am friendly nowadays with a number of Pakistani parents who bring their sons to play in the junior Essex teams. They tend to be more supportive of their children through their innate sense of family than their British counterparts.

On the subject of Pakistan, the upshot of neutral umpires is that I do not foresee any repeat of the Gatting-Shakoor Rana incident in December 1987, that unseemly row between the England captain and the Pakistani official. Many a time in the past, the captain or manager would request that such-and-such an umpire should not stand again, only to find him popping up later in the series. Pakistan's Board of Control would have considered that kind of complaint a slur on its integrity.

In the West Indies in 1973–74, Alan Knott and I managed to save the Third Test with a stand of 142 for the sixth wicket, when I made an unbeaten 129 against the spin of Lance Gibbs and Garry Sobers in conditions that were favourable to them. Ultimately, we drew the series, winning the last Test in Port of Spain, having lost there in the First Test of the series and drawn the others. Greig bowled them out with his hitherto unknown off-cutters, and Boycott, who had not had as successful a tour as Dennis Amiss, made 99 and 112. I recall him saying afterwards that he did not know whether he had done the right thing – winning the match ensured that Denness's time as England captain would be prolonged. That was a measure of his feeling at the time, and he withdrew from Test cricket the following year. I do not think he understood that, even if Denness had been replaced, it would not have been by him. Greig would most probably have been elevated to the captaincy earlier than he was. I would probably have stood a chance as well.

After our travails against Lillee and Thomson in Australia in 1974–75, I made what was to be my highest Test score, 216 in seven hours, in New Zealand at the tailend of that tour. I was averaging in the mid-40s in Test cricket at the time – a successful return by anybody's standards. A few months later, Australia came to England and, on a damp pitch at Edgbaston, beat us in the first of a four-match series. I made the only half-century scored in England's two innings, copying Greig and Knott by cutting the fast bowlers over the slips, but despite this became a scapegoat for defeat, especially in the press. Tony Greig took over the captaincy from Denness and, understandably enough, wanted to bring in different batsmen. With no explanation from the selectors, I was dropped. David Steele took my place and made a remarkable impact. Nowadays, with central contracts in place, that would not happen – individuals bound to the ECB are retained as a unit.

As in 1968 and 1972, when I was chosen again to face Australia, it was at Headingley. This was the infamous Test that was brought to a premature end by saboteurs digging up the pitch in support of George Davis, who was serving a prison term for armed robbery. The match was splendidly poised and I could not believe what I was hearing when I turned on the radio on that fifth morning to be greeted with the news that a gallon of oil had been poured on the surface and chunks dug out of it. I was down at the ground before nine o'clock and realised straight away that there was no chance of any play taking place. The two captains, Greig and Ian Chappell, could have agreed to play on an adjoining strip but that was not likely to happen. So there was little alternative but for the match to be abandoned.

I was upset that, again, I had been given a stormy reception.

It was true that my record at Headingley was not that impressive – and Lillee dismissed me cheaply twice in this match – but the attitude of a number of the spectators appeared to be that only Yorkshiremen were worth supporting or worth consideration for inclusion in the England team. This did get me down. Concentrating and attuning the mind to playing Test cricket was hard enough without having to listen to that. To return to Essex, where increasingly big crowds reflected the improvement of our young team, was something of a relief. My appearances in this series encapsulated my career – play, dropped, play, dropped.

I was chosen for the tour of India in 1976–77 on the basis that I was a more accomplished player of spin than David Steele, and was unlucky to sprain an ankle and be out of action for five weeks. Even when I returned at the end of the series and for the Centenary Test in Australia in 1977, I was not fit. If I had had a more secure place in the middle order, I would probably have had the chance to join Kerry Packer's breakaway World Series Cricket that winter, and I would have had to consider it very seriously as I was coming towards the end of my international career. The likelihood is that I would have signed up. As it was, there was no approach from Greig or anyone else, and it was not in my nature to push myself forward.

On that tour of India, I spent more time with Greig and Amiss, who did sign for Packer, than I did with any other players. I roomed with Greig quite a lot and became godfather to Amiss's son. I could not, though, agree with Greig's viewpoint that World Series Cricket would improve the lot of the average county cricketer. Without the income from Test matches, a number of the first-class counties could have gone out of existence. It seemed to me that argument was a smokescreen to camouflage the fact that the top players were the ones who would thrive. On the other hand, what was not in question was that international players were not well remunerated, given the income we generated. So I understood the criticism at the time but, as it turned out, the good outweighed the harm and the cricketing authorities around the world woke up to the fact that they did not own the leading players. The advent of central contracts, for example, stems indirectly from the contracts and revenue cricketers received from Packer. When Greig decided to emigrate to Australia, I missed him. He loved the big stage and having a good time, although he did not drink much. He had a fine Test record and wanted to carry on playing for England, but this was not feasible given the furore he had created.

As the chance to join Packer slipped by, so, it seemed at the time, did my Test career, in spite of the fact that England lost their best players to World Series Cricket. I regret that I was not a part of the 1978–79 tour under Mike Brearley when England won the Ashes. For that matter, I missed the more arduous trip the following year as well, when the Packer players returned, so did not visit Australia again until I was appointed coach. My main regret now is that I did not play more Test matches during my prime years as a batsman, which were from when I was 27, in 1971, to age 35 in 1979. I had won 52 caps by the time I was dropped in 1977. By the time I was recalled to Test cricket in 1981, I was past my best, although I hoped to remain in the side for the summer of 1982 before passing over the captaincy to someone else. I feel now I would have scored more runs if I had been more selfish and motivated for personal gain. I could have scored, say, 5000 runs at an average of 42 or 43 rather than around 3000 at an average just shy of 40, but I needed a purpose other than just piling up runs for myself. Wanting to win the match, the series or the championship was my motivation. In that I could tolerate eccentricities, I was probably the one member of the England touring parties of my time whom Bernard Thomas, our physio, could put down to share a room with anybody else.

Looking back now, I believe that the main reason why English cricket fell so far behind the game in Australia became apparent in the 1980s. Graham Gooch, John Emburey and Mike Gatting, all prominent Test cricketers, played and learned the game at their state schools in east, south and north London respectively. None of those schools still plays cricket. My old school in Cambridgeshire, which is now a comprehensive, plays a little on account of having an enthusiastic headmaster, but when I was there the game was not a part of the sporting curriculum. It was thought too difficult to organise properly and I played just once in my time there (and was honoured to be made captain). That problem was circumvented by playing village matches and with the help of a teacher who organised net sessions on the concrete surfaces of this former RAF camp. In England, it seemed cricketers of calibre were expected to be unearthed but sufficient thought was not given to where they would come from.

Some of the blame for this was down to the Test and County Cricket Board – now the England and Wales Cricket Board – as well as to the government of the day for selling off school playing fields. Clubs needed to be encouraged to take over the role of schools and, indeed, they have started to do this now by taking on and fielding youngsters. However, I think it should be made standard practice that if any club wants to participate in any league in England, it has to run a youth side. In Australia, where there is little football by comparison, every school plays the national sport – the upshot being highly competitive matches between schools in Sydney. I don't imagine they bother about laying on any tea.

Only success is rewarded in Australia. That is their culture whereas ours is a culture of expectation. State cricketers who are dropped play in grade one cricket, for which they are not paid. There is no sizeable staff of players, as exists in county cricket. Test players are not given sponsored cars by their clubs and under-performing, unfit players are not tolerated, as has happened in England. The question of lacklustre players has vexed the first-class counties to the point that more performance-related salaries, such as Sussex introduced so successfully when they took on Mushtaq Ahmed, are going to have to come into vogue. As for the Australia Academy, which was an obvious innovation long before any thought was given to having one in England, this became a finishing school for the best players from all the states. It is not difficult to see how the game there prospered, while, for a good number of years, ours stagnated.

CHAPTER 2

COACHING TRIALS

Long-standing friends warned me against becoming England coach. Micky Stewart, who had the distinction of becoming the first person to hold that position and whose approach to the game was markedly similar to mine, was not keen to continue in the post and tour India in 1992–93. He was intent on taking up a post with the Test and County Cricket Board. I was told I was first choice to succeed him, ahead of Norman Gifford, the former England spinner who went on to coach Sussex, and, perhaps, Jack Birkenshaw, whose coaching was to make such an impression on Leicestershire. This did not mean much to Doug Insole and David Acfield, who had long been confidants and administrative and playing colleagues with Essex. They impressed upon me that I would not enjoy the political ramifications of the job or the media interest and speculation that was by now such a major aspect of it. I could, and perhaps should, have remained with the county. The salary offered by the TCCB was not in itself much of an incentive, yet I well knew that the opportunity to coach at national level would not come again.

I also knew from long observation of cricketing standards around the country that it would be at least five years before England had a competitive side once more. In fact, that was to prove an underestimation. So rather than accept the three-year contract that was on offer, I made it clear that I would not take on the position for any less than five. Frank Chamberlain, the then chairman of the TCCB, and A.C. Smith, the chief executive, acquiesced and gave me a five-year contract at £50,000 a year. This was to prove a contentious issue in due course when I was dismissed and I was very glad I had that security.

What difference did I feel I could make when Micky Stewart had had enough? Although I knew it wasn't going to be an easy task, I did truly believe I could turn England into a better team. Stewart had been fortunate in being able to select Mike Gatting, David Gower and Graham Gooch when they were relatively young; they were past their prime years when I took over. The same could be said of Allan Lamb and Robin Smith and, of the bowlers, Angus 'Gus' Fraser (because of injury) and Phil DeFreitas. I knew that I would have to contend with a period of significant change and I was far from certain that their replacements would be of Test standard, but I still felt I could make a positive difference.

Having coached Essex for five seasons, I was aware of where to draw the line of demarcation between my duties and the prerogative of the captain. It was essential that both should be speaking with one voice, in public if not necessarily in private. I felt that, as well as determining never to criticise the captain in public, I should always support whatever decision he chose to make, be this a declaration or leaving a particular player out of the team. Although I had led Essex (and England) without the support of a first-team coach, I had always benefited from the full backing of my county's cricket committee. It was right that the captain should take the plaudits.

Although I resolved also to support the players whenever possible, as I would have expected had someone been in authority over me, I realised there would be times when I would not be able to fool the media or defend the indefensible. I knew some of the journalists better than the England players did. Friendships had been forged during the long hours spent together in hotels and airport lounges and restaurants. I knew whom to trust, but there was bound to be a limit to the number of off-the-record briefings I could give. There comes a time when it is not possible to keep on making excuses.

I felt my knowledge could be put to best use working on a one-to-one basis. I prefer that, anyway, to addressing a crowded room, as I found out when I first undertook public speaking. I enjoy discussions with enthusiastic players over where to bowl and the safest areas in which to score runs. On the other hand, I believed firmly, as Mike Brearley did before me, that England players had reached the level they were at through knowing how to play. He did not encourage Kenny Barrington, in his capacity as England tour manager, to spend too much time dissecting players' techniques. I felt I should not tamper overmuch and should impress upon them that they must back themselves. My task was to improve them if I possibly could and to assist with their concerns and woes. The most trying aspect of the job turned out to be interruptions to placate sponsors, even when I was supposed to be supervising net practice. I was unprepared for that, and sponsors' demands, understandable because of their financial commitments, became far too time-consuming.

Wisden declared that I had a tendency towards fatalism and pessimism. The observations of others can sometimes highlight characteristics we do not see in ourselves, but if *Wisden* was right, that tendency can be dated back to the start of my first tour as coach, which began on a downbeat note and never improved. Gooch, the captain, who decided to come to India only because this was my initial trip, told me at the airport that his marriage was over. He had met Brenda at a young age and they had grown apart, but I had no inkling of this previously and neither had any of the Essex team. Our conversation was overheard by a journalist and the story was in the *Daily Mirror* the next day. He was still our best batsman, one of England's finest cricketers, even though he was coming to the end of his career, but he struggled thereafter mentally as well as physically. He had stomach trouble, flu bugs and did not go on to Sri Lanka for the last leg of the tour.

Then there were the differences between him and David Gower. I had put Gower's name down for the tour and there is no doubt that he would have made runs, but Gooch and the other selectors did not want to take him. Their approach to the game was wholly different from Gower's, and he did not fit into an era of intensified net practice and training in the gym. He would have given us something on the field, if nothing off it. He could sometimes be a bit of a disruptive influence, making smart arse comments and being flippant at team meetings – which I could never understand other than to take it as an attempt at humour and to keep people at arm's length.

Throughout my years as Essex captain, I had been permitted to have the team I wanted and hence to quibble with Gooch now would have gone against my ingrained notion of selection. I did not wish to contradict him and do not believe he had too much influence at the time. Nevertheless, I should still have insisted on taking Gower, although we were going to a country where touring was invariably difficult and it was necessary for the party to stick together.

Phil Tufnell was one who couldn't hack it. He seemed to have no idea how people lived in India and didn't wish to analyse their modes of survival. He appeared to be suffering from depression and yet was hyperactive. His mood swings could extend to feeling suicidal. What he did enjoy, even though he was not in the same class as the Indian spinners, was his bowling. He was in what might be termed the second division of Test bowlers, but nonetheless was the best English slow bowler of his day. Tufnell did not crack jokes and if he made you laugh, it was down to him being peculiar more than funny. I watched him winning 'I'm a Celebrity – Get Me Out of Here!' and my immediate reaction was that he was one of the last people I would have expected to succeed in the jungle. The public took to him because they regarded him as a likeable rogue. He could easily have fitted into the existence of the rag and bone man I encountered in the East End in my youth.

After the first week in India, Tufnell wanted to go home. In addition to his problems, and Gooch's, Mike Gatting and John Emburey – important, experienced players – were not well. When Emburey was fit to bowl his off-spin, Sidhu kept hitting him out of the ground and he lost confidence, conceded a large number of runs in one Test and was then ill. Our other main slow bowler, Ian Salisbury, bowled too many loose balls, as he did throughout his career, although every pitch took spin. He could not afford that against good players.

We lost the First Test, Gooch's one hundredth, although he was not well enough to celebrate or excel in it, by eight wickets. Our attack comprised Devon Malcolm, Paul Jarvis, Chris Lewis, Paul Taylor and Salisbury, none of whom would have commanded a place had they played a decade later. The pollution level was so marked that Ted Dexter, as chairman of selectors, commissioned a special study. I never discovered the findings and suspect that not a great deal could have been done about it, anyway. Preparation against the kind of leg spin we would encounter was difficult enough without trying to acclimatise the players to the atmosphere as well.

On the eve of the Second Test in Madras, Gooch and Gatting ate a Chinese meal, usually the safest food you can obtain in India, in our hotel, including an extra plate of prawns, and were ill that night. The press came to the conclusion that the prawns were responsible but in reality the players could have picked up any kind of bug or food poisoning. The upshot was that one dropped out of the match altogether and the other had to leave the field and contributed two low scores. We lost the match by an innings, which was no less of a sound defeat than the First Test.

Gooch scored all too few runs during the series but ultimately that was just one of any number of problems. One of the worst was an air pilots' strike, which meant we had to travel around by train. Bob Bennett, our manager who became a good friend of mine, had to sort out a number of complicated journeys. We were stuck for eighteen hours on one train and had to play a Test the next day. When we eventually arrived at our destination, we were exhausted but a photograph of our dishevelled group that had been wired back to England led to condemnatory comments about dress and shaving. No account was taken of the fact that this was not exactly an inter-city sleeper. It would not, of course, have been an issue had we been winning the major matches. Some Australian sides in my time were far from smartly turned out and Ian Chappell and Mike Brearley would not have tolerated any admonishments over their dress and not shaving. I recall Mike Selvey, when he played under Brearley, not even bothering to wear shoes.

Some of my players in India barely had the strength to shave, anyway. In not one of those Tests did we have half our team fit. We finished up losing all three, India winning the Third Test in spite of Graeme Hick making 178, and then being beaten in Sri Lanka as well. Gooch was not at all sure he wanted to continue as captain and the uncertainty, heightened by the inevitable difficulties caused by his marriage breakdown, continued for some weeks.

A tour to the Indian sub-continent was harder even than playing in Australia – it was the most arduous trip to undertake, as is probably still the case today. The pollution in Calcutta was such that the sun did not appear until 3 p.m. and some players could not breathe properly. The air was foul in Bombay and Madras, too, in addition to the fierce heat. On top of all this, our batsmen were not so well prepared to play spin as on my tours as a player in 1972–73 and 1976–77 because they were less accustomed to batting on turning pitches in county cricket. I played in those conditions in Essex once a week in the 1960s but by 1993 we had suffered ten years of bland pitches in England and hence did not know how to play high-class spinners. That said, I had watched Anil Kumble bowl in South Africa before the tour and reckoned he would take wickets only if the conditions were in his favour. Unfortunately, compared to my previous visit to India in 1981–82, when I was captain of England, they were. The three pitches were cut so as to bring about a positive result, which was certainly not the case in the Gavaskar era, eleven years earlier.

Cricket followers, by and large, do not understand what it is like to tour the sub-continent. Not long after returning home, I drove a considerable way to play in a benefit match for Derek Randall and was given some terrible stick from the Nottinghamshire crowd, which made me realise how fickle the British public can be. I had given up a Sunday afternoon to raise funds for one of their players, an old England colleague of mine, but with hindsight I should have kept out of the way. On other occasions I had the headlights of my car kicked in at Edgbaston and was spat at and had items thrown at me from a pub just outside Headingley, which was sited adjacent to traffic lights. I drove away from the ground in a different direction after that, but visiting it continued to be an unpleasant experience owing to abuse from drunks on the Western Terrace. Players' guests had to sit among the general public, which was far from ideal, and it was not long before Sue could see that the job was wearing me down and felt I should give it up, although she kept her thoughts to herself – and this was all before we had undertaken a tour to Australia.

Australia were the visitors in 1993 and again we suffered seemingly intractable difficulties. By the end of the summer, Gooch had given up the captaincy, having given me no warning that he was about to do so. He felt, not unreasonably, that he could no longer motivate the players. To have been coach or manager, call it what you will, when he and Gatting were at their peak would have made a great difference. The fact that they were still our best batsmen at this final stage of their careers said too much about the English game. The fundamental reason for Australia's triumph against us in 1993, which they repeated on our winter tour eighteen months later, was that they possessed superior players. That is not to say nothing could have been done about it but, as has been stressed often enough over the last fifteen years or so, any England team has needed to be performing at its absolute peak to compete with them. Ever since Allan Border revitalised their team at the end of the 1980s, captaining and coaching Australia have been exceedingly straightforward tasks.

The essential difference between the two countries in the 1990s, as had been the case when I played against them in the 1970s, was the presence of two exceptional bowlers. Dennis Lillee and Jeff Thomson were succeeded in due course by Shane Warne and Glenn McGrath, although McGrath did not play against us in the 1993 series. The sheer number of wickets that these two have taken has meant that the captain has been able to give more concentration to other areas of the game. In time, with other high-class batsmen and fielders in the team, too, Steve Waugh could risk losing wickets in pursuit of quick runs because he knew he could bring on match-winning performers whenever the opposition was in the ascendancy.

Australian captains have always been responsible for team selection and running the game on the field. Bobby Simpson, coach in the Border era of the late eighties, would work out fielding drills and give talks at team meetings. He had a considerable knowledge of the game, a work ethic and a sense of purpose, but above all he was running a group of talented and self-motivated cricketers. He had great experience of playing at Test level, and had the ability to read a game well so he could advise Border and, later, Mark Taylor on where to bowl. He could also pick out weaknesses in the opposition and did not frown on someone having a drink and enjoying themselves, so long as this was within reason. He was a very confident bloke who particularly liked talking about how good a cricketer he had been and what a great job he did when he returned to captain Australia in the Packer era.

By comparison, I do not believe John Buchanan, his successor, has contributed much, if anything, to Australia's triumphs. There is a balance to be struck between analysing a batsman through a video camera and computer, and analysing him in the nets. When Buchanan spent an ill-fated season as coach of Middlesex, the Test cricketers in that side did not think he devoted enough time to working on technique. If I had received one of his pamphlets about Zen or Buddhism under my door, I would not have bothered to read it. I would have regarded it as a joke and I cannot see it motivating McGrath or Warne or their colleagues. Those players are experienced enough to know what is required of them.

Older Middlesex and England cricketers, such as Mike Gatting and Mark Ramprakash, found Buchanan's approach too modernistic, although I fully believe that analysing every ball a bowler delivers and every run a batsman scores has its place. Bob Woolmer has shown in his time as coach of Warwickshire, South Africa and Pakistan how a batsman's game can be improved using on-screen techniques in conjunction with net practice, but a coach who spends all day in front of a laptop cannot observe the whole picture unfolding in front of him.

In addition, I am not sure how much Buchanan knows about the game. I am still a firm believer in employing specialist coaches who excel in different areas – fast and spin bowling, wicket-keeping, fielding. As far as I am concerned, such specialists are more important than sports psychologists. Having said that, I also think that sports psychologists have a role to play and are worth employing if they can squeeze just another 1 per cent from players in terms of achievement. When I was England coach, Ramprakash consulted Mike Brearley in his capacity as a psychoanalyst. Who knows, perhaps I would have benefited from seeing one in my own playing days. I would have benefited still more from being able to consult a coach.

Bobby Simpson inherited some top-class players, the game was the national sport and it was buoyant at school and club level, and in those things he was fortunate. In England in 1993, there were no such advantages. Cricket was being downgraded in state schools and football had become the dominant sport among all age groups and in the media. Around a third of county cricketers had combined both sports in years gone by at amateur or professional level, but football was by now a year-round activity so such players were lost forever to what had once been called the summer game. The Neville brothers of Manchester United, both talented sportsmen, would not have needed to give much consideration to whether their futures lay in football or with Lancashire CCC. They were soon earning vast sums. Parents were given signing-on fees to attract their sons to Premier League and other league clubs, and Essex lost two or three potential cricketers each year to the lure of football. I could not advise parents against making that choice. What it amounted to was that a depressingly thin layer of talent was emerging in the first-class game and it was self-evident that England's Test team was as weak as it can ever have been.

When I returned to Test cricket as coach in 1992–93, I soon learned that the game in Australia at the highest level – indeed, probably at every level – had moved on apace. Border was coming to the end of his career, having done an immense amount for his country. Taylor, a decent man, had succeeded him by the time we toured Australia in 1994–95 and soon proved to be an even more astute captain. With Ian Healy as wicket-keeper, and Mark and Steve Waugh and Warne in the slips, the advice he received was sound. Steve Waugh, dour and determined, with a lot of Boycott's grittiness and refusal to surrender his wicket about him, epitomised the Australian outlook. Some people are motivated by figures, by the accumulation of runs, and he was one of them. He talked, as many of them did, about pride in his country and how much representing it meant to him. The impression I formed was that sport meant more to the nation as a whole, and indeed had greater status, than in England.

The essential point was that all of their players were Australian. Over the years, more than a few England players have learned their cricket abroad – for example, Tony Greig, Allan Lamb, Graeme Hick, Andy Caddick, Chris Smith and Robin Smith and, in due course, Kevin Pietersen. South Africans could not play Test cricket in apartheid South Africa and, post-apartheid, they were aware more money was on offer in England. When I was coach, Robin Smith was one of the few batsmen who was likely to make runs consistently but he was not always focused on his game. He had business interests and was also a party-goer. Even if players had lived in England from a young age, some did not necessarily identify with it. National identity was being watered down. Greig, one of my best friends in the game, was an exception, a fine, whole-hearted all-rounder, and one of the better players England have ever been able to select. No one could ever say that he did not give his all, but I wonder to what extent we would have been worse off without these individuals.

The 1993 series, which Australia won 4–1 over six Tests, is best remembered now for the emergence of Warne, and in particular the ball with which he dismissed Gatting at Old Trafford. This had a marked effect on the dressing room and, fine bowler though he already was, made Warne into an ogre, fuelling the idea that he was a better spinner than was the reality. Had Gatting been in for longer or known more about this new 'leggie' who carried no particular reputation before him at the time, he might well have padded the ball away. He did not get into the best position to play it, opening himself up too much to the leg side. No one expected it to turn two feet after it had drifted in, and it hit the top of the off stump. Gatting, a fine player of spin, returned to the pavilion with a downtrodden air about him and others in the team understandably felt that, if he could not cope with Warne, they would not be able to do so, either.

Warne, like Ian Botham, comes up with a great many ideas on a cricket field. Some are laudable, others woolly. He, too, has great confidence in his own ability, which occasionally, as evidenced in his Hampshire captaincy, can result in over-exuberance. I regard him as highly as any leg-spinner I have seen or played against, with the possible exception of Abdul Qadir of Pakistan, who was at his peak for a short period – eighteen months – in the early 1980s. Qadir was a bit quicker through the air than Warne and possessed a little more variation. Warne does not bowl many googlies, perhaps because of his shoulder trouble, but he has remained remarkably consistent for a long period and has been a far better bowler than the foremost leg-spinners of my playing days, John Gleeson, Intikhab Alam and Robin Hobbs.

If I had batted against Warne, I would have tried to read him out of the hand and worked out when he was likely to bowl his flipper. He and his kind are often bowlers of habit. If, for example, he was hit to the boundary off the back foot through the covers, he often followed that up with the flipper because it gave the appearance of a ball of the same length. His googly is apparent because it is thrown up more than his leg-break and pitches outside off stump. I would have tried to out-think him and to pick his length, which any good player of spin has to be able to do, and to upset his line by slog-sweeping him. I might have tried to go down the pitch and hit him through wide mid-on, on the full, or feint to come down the pitch and not do so. I did not think that the sledging in the 1993 series was any worse than it had been before, but I told my England players not to become involved in any backchat with him unless they could answer back without their game being affected.

I would have liked to play against Warne. I would have reckoned to make the most of conditions that were favourable for batting. He would have got me out, for sure, but in-between times I'd have made runs against him on good pitches. We did watch him on video and dissected his method of attack, but that did not necessarily make a jot of difference. We discussed methods of combating his flipper in the First Test of the 1994–95 series in Brisbane, only for Alec Stewart immediately to mis-read it and be bowled. Warne took eight for 71 in that innings and, as coach, I had to take the criticism rather than the batsmen concerned, who had been versed in what to expect. By then, lesser players – not Atherton, Gooch or Stewart – conceivably were cowed by Warne. Gooch, who also, interestingly enough, rated Qadir more highly, could read him fairly well and, although not technically correct against spinners, always tried to bully them. He could play Warne better than anybody. The problem was that others, particularly the tailenders, were blown away by him and the other exceptional spin bowler of the period, Muttiah Muralitharan.

Warne also indulged in a certain amount of kidology. Before every tour, he would announce that he had developed a mystery ball. This was rubbish. There is nothing mysterious about something he calls 'a slider'. It is merely a leg spinner that does not turn. There is no such delivery as 'a zooter'. More rubbish. Warne possesses a fine variation of pace and length and his most dangerous ball, without any question, is his leg spinner. This is also his stock ball. The most important thing when facing him is to play the ball and not the man. Even the best bowlers can bowl you one that is short or off line and no batsman can afford to allow a bowler of his quality to bowl on his terms. Left-handers – and again we should have chosen Gower to combat him in 1993 – have more of a chance because they can sweep him with the spin. Brian Lara, Graham Thorpe and Marcus Trescothick try to do so, as would Matthew Hayden and Justin Langer if they were playing against him. All credit to those who run the Australian Academy for criticising Warne initially for being a slob. That proved to be the making of him and his presence was the single most significant factor in his country's triumph in that summer of 1993.

Australia won the first two Tests, at Old Trafford and Lord's, which meant that the first six matches under my control had all ended in defeat. It was not as if they were closely contested, either. As in India and Sri Lanka, the margins were considerable – 179 runs in one and an innings and 62 runs in the other. Border was making runs and capitalising on the knowledge he had acquired when playing for Essex. The same could be said of Mark Waugh and Merv Hughes. I believe that they were as much benefit to us as we were to them, but if there was an argument to be had over whether or not overseas players should be permitted to take part in the County Championship, now was the time to have it. The particular concern of the media, though, was more to do with the lack of emerging talent coupled with our poor results.

After Australia had won the Ashes in the Fourth Test at Headingley, Gooch, although still a prolific batsman, decided he had 'no more petrol in the tank', as he put it, and resigned the captaincy. He continued to play, though, and made two decent scores in our victory in the last Test of the series at The Oval. One more fall-out was that Ted Dexter, with whom I had played in my first Test and who had been a conscientious chairman of selectors, took responsibility for our series defeat and resigned. He came across badly to the public, who must have thought he was a bit batty, and he could be naïve, but that was part of his charm. His announcement at an earlier press conference that Micky Stewart, England coach at the time, had stuck up for his son Alec to become England captain was a case in point, as was his famous comment, 'Who could forget Malcolm Devon?' His choices for selection were generally sound, although in 1993 he held a theory that Mark Lathwell would succeed as a Test batsman. Conceivably, Dexter had an affinity with that kind of dashing style and, in terms of raw talent, this was a fair choice. Less apparent was evidence of a desire to play Test cricket and to cope with the attendant pressures. Alas, after two disappointing matches Lathwell returned to Somerset and dropped out of the game altogether in due course.

The England players who did not know Dexter well thought he was barking mad. He would arrive at the team hotel in leathers and helmet on a smart motorbike, preceding his stunning wife, who would arrive in more conventional style. The doorman, not knowing whether he was James Bond or some yobbo, would be bemused. Those who came to know him, including Gooch, Atherton and me, had great affection for him. We were aware that he belonged more to the era of Denis Compton, Bill Edrich and Keith Miller than to an age when the media would swoop on indiscreet comments, and gambling was not in vogue. I don't think Dexter came to terms with changed times and a more acerbic media.

In 1993, we were up against players who possessed a sense of pride in themselves and their country and who were, in several instances, world-class performers to boot, and we had few means of contending with them. I was aware, for example, of how to bowl at Steve Waugh, but there was a divergence of views. Short-pitched bowling did not get him out as Michael

Atherton, for one, thought for a while that it would. Waugh would move out of the way and fend the ball off rather than attempt to hook it. The right approach was to deliver the ball just outside off stump, of full length, moving into or away from the bat, but the drawback was that we did not have the bowlers capable of doing that. If I had had Darren Gough or Andy Caddick, or for that matter Andy Flintoff, I would have brought him on straight away, rather than allowing Waugh to play himself into form against the spinners. Curiously enough, Waugh liked to play a few shots as soon as he went in, flailing at anything outside off stump, and then, when he had settled down, consolidate in that customarily efficient way, making his runs with compact, crisp, short-arm shots punched away to the on side by comparison with his brother's more flowery style. Steve conned many bowlers into bowling too short to him and he scored a considerable number of crucial runs when batting with tailenders, although he did not protect the tail that much and rarely lost his wicket in such circumstances. He could have farmed the bowling a lot more than he did but he liked being not out. He was a more effective batsman than his brother and was on a par with Border, Greg Chappell and Ricky Ponting. His figures don't lie.

I knew Mark Waugh much better, of course, through his association with Essex. He was not as technically tight a player as his brother. As a batsman who went for his shots, he could be dismissed that much more readily, but he was capable of playing some valuable innings on indifferent pitches, as he did at Edgbaston in 1993, when the ball turned square. He played some crucial one-day innings, opening the batting for Australia, and was not at all selfish, being prepared to sacrifice his wicket for the team. If his captain needed 40 runs in six overs before making a declaration, he would have a go.

I'm not sure Steve would do the same in similar circumstances. Mark would lose his wicket when batting with the
tail but would make 20 or 30 runs quicker than Steve did in
such circumstances. He was quiet and drank little, although
he was sociable with a good sense of humour, but he found
media interviews a chore. When he played for Essex, he had
a love-hate relationship with Nasser Hussain. They would be
having lunch together at Chelmsford and he would say,
'Playing for yourself again, Nass?' to which, of course, Hussain
would fire back a suitable retort.

Other significant Australian cricketers at this time included
David Boon, a back-foot player who was strong off his legs and
pulled and hooked. He always had to be prised out. Not a
batsman who possessed devastating shots or whom spectators
would travel a long way to watch, Boon was the kind every
team needed to offset those with greater flamboyance. He was
also a fine bat–pad fielder. Then there was Ian Healy, who kept
wicket really well to Warne and Tim May. He did not miss
many chances. You would never have thought that he would
be competent enough to go in at number seven, because he was
unorthodox, but having a good eye made him effective.

Others appeared better than they were because they were
playing in a winning team. May was one. A decent but not
outstanding off-spinner, he generally pitched the ball outside
off stump, and bowled with five fielders on the off side and
four on the leg side. He was not as hard to play as the Indian
spinners Prasanna or Venkataraghavan, to name two fine
bowlers of my day, but he was of a standard that opposing
batsmen should expect to play at Test level. The drawback
was that England batsmen had seen all too little decent spin
bowling in county cricket, and then on covered and bland
pitches, and we accorded him too much respect. Our batsmen

should have tried to hit him off his length. Robin Smith, for one, gave him too much credit. Smith was a far better player of spin than most of the others but he read too many newspapers and listened to what every media pundit was saying. Smith should have been capable of bullying spinners in the way that Gooch did.

Craig McDermott was the pick of the fast bowlers before McGrath came to the fore. McDermott had to return home after two Tests on the 1993 tour due to injury, but he excelled against us on the 1994–95 trip. He bowled at between 83 and 86mph, which was a decent pace, and shaped the ball away from the right-hander. He did not make it swing a great deal but he could bowl consistently on a length. I should imagine McGrath modelled himself on McDermott, although McGrath was a bit taller, gained more bounce and learned to reverse swing the ball into right-handers, and his bouncer was always directed where it should be, namely at the batsman's throat. McGrath depended on seam, accuracy – he would have Michael Atherton lbw on the crease, not properly forward or back – a good yorker and a bouncer. He did not swing the ball as much as, say, Richard Hadlee but he was a good catcher in the deep and possessed a fine arm, although that could be taken as the norm for Australians. He has certainly been as effective as Courtney Walsh, if not a better bowler.

In so far as matching like for like was concerned, we just could not compete, with one exception. Gus Fraser, had he been fit, would have made a significant difference. He returned, after two and a half years out of Test cricket due to a hip injury, for the final Test of the 1993 series at The Oval and took eight wickets. As he amply demonstrated, he was the only bowler of any quality we possessed, even though he had lost half a yard of pace, bowling at between 79 and 80mph as opposed to 84 to 85mph in his pomp, and was not quite the performer he had been before. The upshot was that we won the match, although we were greatly helped by the pressure being off the Australians. Winning the last match of a series we had lost was becoming a habit.

Having been heavily beaten in 1993, we were defeated 3-1 in Australia eighteen months later. I did not feel the matches were as one-sided as that statistic suggests. Given a little good fortune and the odd umpiring decision going our way, we could have won the last three Tests. Once again, a tour began inauspiciously. Devon Malcolm, who had bowled out South Africa so memorably in our last Test of the summer of 1994, went down with chickenpox before the start of the series. He had illustrated then that he could be a match-winner and Atherton handled him as well as anyone could have done. Lovely bloke and good time-keeper though he was, no one could get through to Devon. If he was told a particular batsman was weak against short-pitched bowling, he'd pitch the ball up. Sometimes he had a vacant look about him and I wondered whether he had taken in the advice Geoff Arnold, our fast-bowling coach, and I had given him. He bowled what are known in the game as wicket-taking balls when he followed through properly and did not fall away at the crease, but he could be hit all round the ground. When he was playing, someone disciplined, such as Fraser, had to bowl at the other end. Malcolm was a one-dimensional modern-day cricketer and it was hard for the captain to decide whether to under-attack or over-attack with his field placings when giving him the ball. Atherton got it right most of time.

Players always look for a crutch when they lose form and Malcolm was to blame Arnold and me, saying that we gave him conflicting advice over whether to bowl fast or to cut down his pace and concentrate on trying to make the ball swing. My belief now is that he gave his utmost and achieved all he could without possessing anything like the talent of say, Chris Lewis. I admit that I lost my temper with both of them on occasion. Of the two, Lewis had so much more ability, but ultimately was not worth his place. He could bat and was a decent fielder, but he would always bowl better and quicker at people whom he thought he could dismiss. He rarely removed good players because he didn't run in at them with sufficient purpose. It seemed to me that he did not possess the self-belief to succeed and, like Lathwell, he eventually dropped out of the game altogether. I have no idea what he is doing now.

In the First Test in Brisbane, when Malcolm had chickenpox, which he picked up from Joey Benjamin, our opening attack was Phil DeFreitas and Martin McCague, which probably constituted the weakest new-ball pair in the history of matches between the two countries. They conceded 26 runs off the first four overs through long hops and balls wide of the leg stump. Australia had the initiative they required and they were never going to lose it, not least because we could not keep the fast bowlers fit. Darren Gough and McCague, who did not have the personality to take the stick meted out to him by the Australian press and public, had ailments of one sort or another. I could never work out why Ray Illingworth, when chairman of selectors, did not appreciate the ability of Fraser, who, when fit, should have been his ideal cricketer because he was gutsy and a keen trier. Illingworth could not get on with him and didn't think his medium pace was suited to Australian conditions. DeFreitas was a better bowler than, say, Max Walker, but he was not a front-line bowler. We simply could not dismiss Australia cheaply, with the exception of when Gough took six for 49 to bowl them out for 116 in the Third

Test in Sydney and when Malcolm took four wickets to bring about victory in the Fourth Test in Adelaide.

In addition to dealing with Malcolm, I had to contend with Graeme Hick, whose game had been affected by both mental and technical shortcomings that for a long time had been obscured by the sheer weight of runs he scored in county cricket. Here, I had more success. In fact, I think I got more out of him than anyone else succeeded in doing. I felt he had as much ability as any batsman in the team and, had I carried on as England coach, I think his overall batting average would have been nearer 45 than 31, which would have reflected his talent. His average was well below that of most batsmen who have played Test cricket for as long as he did. His technical weakness was that he could not lift his hands high enough back past his body in his pick-up, which resulted in his having difficulty against the short-pitched ball on middle or middle and leg stump. The West Indies spotted this immediately and as a result he struggled against their fast bowlers in his first series in Test cricket. Hick was quiet and pleasant but not a tremendous mixer. On tour it is necessary to make friends and go out with county colleagues and others.

Hick needed others, particularly those in authority, to have confidence in him. If he felt they doubted his ability, he could not give his all for them. Unfortunately, not one of his captains, Gooch, Atherton or Hussain, had total belief in him – and they did not keep their doubts to themselves. Gooch and, for that matter, Gatting, were not overkeen on picking cricketers who were from other countries and Hick, who was born in Zimbabwe, would have been aware of this. He needed to feel wanted in order to perform and I think the captains whom he played under should have tried harder to make him feel appreciated. Plenty of players with worse technical faults have scored more runs than him, but his game was affected. It was also affected by too much batting practice against the bowling machine in the nets, and the ball being thrown down to him in similarly mechanical fashion. This was too robotic a form of practice for him, which should have been picked up early in his career. By the time I came to coach him, it was too late to sort this out – the whole rhythm of his game had been affected. In county cricket, few bowlers, if any, were capable of making the ball rise up to chest height from the back of a length, and he benefited accordingly.

On that 1994–95 tour, Hick averaged 41.60 in the Test series, batting at number three, before he slipped a disc and missed the last two matches. The worst decision Atherton made as captain in my time was to declare in the Third Test in Sydney when Hick was on 98, having blocked three balls in succession. I think for the sake of another over or two, he should have been allowed to reach his century. At the time, Atherton was talking with Gooch and might have been influenced by his thoughts. Hick should have been given more specific instructions and not scratched around as he did, but he was too sensitive over the whole issue. Atherton did not consult me over his declaration, which I was somewhat peeved about, but still Hick hardly spoke to me for a month, particularly at breakfast time which, for a coach, was extremely trying. He thought I was party to this decision and I never disabused him because I felt I had to stand by the captain's declaration – there has to appear to be unity between the two central figures. My successors, David Lloyd and Duncan Fletcher, have shown the worth of that in recent years.

I could never comprehend the mindset of coaches and managers who make personal and public criticism of their charges. This was not confined to Ray Illingworth. Ray Jennings of South Africa is a prime example of an individual whose motivational methods I didn't agree with. Encouraging one of his bowlers to hit Allan Donald on the head in the nets was just plain stupidity, as were his comments about what he perceived to be the weaknesses of senior players such as Jacques Kallis and Herschelle Gibbs. I believe such remarks should be confined to the dressing room and not played out through the media. If players are experiencing indifferent form, the coach's job is to assist them. Goodness knows what Jennings would have made of Hick and said about him. I noticed that when his South African team was struggling in the field, they appeared very flat.

I felt that whatever Atherton did or said, I had to appear supportive. We did not always agree but we usually worked in consultation. If he asked me to take a particular practice, I would do so. If I suggested something, he would act upon it. I think we both felt that Hick should have succeeded to a greater extent than he did in Test cricket. Had he continued to play county cricket and waited for Zimbabwe to gain Test status, it is conceivable he would now be regarded as a batsman of high standing, if not a great batsman, as Barry Richards is today, even though his ability was not properly put to the test in international cricket. Yet on this tour and in the Caribbean the previous winter, Hick's game had not progressed in a way that all commentators thought it would. His inability to make more of his talent was one of the frustrations of my period as coach and has been an abiding sore point ever since because I felt I understood his capabilities and his character – but my time was up before his.

Frustratingly, although the declaration in that Third Test had not been delayed to allow Hick to reach his century, we still could not win. Having begun with a double century opening stand, Australia's middle order collapsed to the extent that they had just three wickets remaining and no chance of making 449 to win, but the light faded and we ran out of time. We had lost the Second Test by as crushing a margin as the First and desperately needed a victory. Darren Gough had done all he could to bring it about by taking six wickets for 49 in Australia's first innings. He was the find of the tour and struck me immediately as the kind of positive, bullish trier we needed in the dressing room. Like Fred Trueman, he always thought he could take a wicket. Like Fred, too, indeed like most Yorkshiremen of that era, he was always talking about himself. He was the kind of infectious character any captain would want to have in his team and in the dressing room and I believe he would have played for England in any period. He could swing the ball away from the bat and learned to reverse swing it on coarse pitches. If he was not as good as John Snow, whose tally of wickets he overtook towards the end of his Test career, he was still, in 2005, a better bet than Jon Lewis to have taken to South Africa as a stand-in bowler. Whether or not he thought he had played Test cricket for the last time, he would have been on the plane if asked to go. It is always best in such circumstances to send for the person the opposition would least like to see.

Still, we managed to win the Fourth Test, even though Gough returned home as the result of a foot injury at the very time when he was making a significant impression. We were down to just eleven fit players. Gatting had struggled in Australia so a century by him now, scratchy though it was, said much about his character and determination to show he could still bat. It was a fitting swansong. He and Gooch were to retire from international cricket at the end of this series and, at their ages, you could see why. Yet who, other than Atherton and possibly Stewart, was any better? Graham Thorpe was not yet established and John Crawley did not fulfil the flourishing career that had been expected of him. Malcolm, rather than Fraser, won us this match by taking seven wickets but, rather like his form, success turned out to be illusory – another consolation victory. Stung by this defeat, Australia won the final Test of the series at Perth by another overwhelming margin.

We collapsed in our second innings to 123 all out in decent batting conditions. It is true that a quick pitch with good carry suited McDermott, who moved the ball away from the bat and took six wickets for 38, but he was not, by then, as quick as he once was – around 85mph – and his injuries and lack of enthusiasm for touring was such that his career did not extend beyond that year. McGrath was just taking wing at that stage. Ominously, he had Atherton out for two low scores in this match, both times caught by the wicket-keeper. It was a portent of what was to come.

Despite the defeat, I still clung to the notion that as we had put ourselves into a position to draw the series, I would still be coaching England come the summer. At no stage, even when we capitulated on that last day, did I feel I had made my last contribution to international cricket. I was, no doubt, naïve. As Michael Atherton said later, there is a finite time for a coach to be in charge of a losing team. The saddest aspect of not continuing in the post was that my partnership with him also came to an end.

CHAPTER 3

BEING CAPTAIN

When it came to choosing between Michael Atherton and Alec Stewart to succeed Graham Gooch in the summer of 1993, I thought back to the various England captains I had known to try to determine the qualities that made them preeminent or, in one or two cases, not as well suited to the position. When I first played Test cricket, I found Colin Cowdrey to be a well-meaning person who struggled to contend with adversity in Pakistan in 1969, and leaned on Les Ames, the manager, to hold the team together. Ray Illingworth and Tony Greig were diametrically opposed – tactical expertise was not matched by man-management skills and vice versa. Tony Lewis had to cope with a long tour of the sub-continent in 1972–73 and did so by using his charm and tact. Mike Denness's forte was in the one-day game. The qualities inherent in the leadership of Alec's father, Micky, were such that I felt him to be the finest captain I played under and, for that reason alone, I listened carefully when he advocated Alec as England captain, but I knew him to be wrong.

There was little purpose in arguing with Graham Gooch over his decision to resign the England captaincy towards the end of that long summer of 1993. Once his mind was made up over a particular issue he could be steadfast, and he felt he was not making any headway with England players who were not responding to his promptings. Who, then, should succeed him? Should we revert to Mike Gatting, whose abilities were well documented in the game, as were his foibles. Why not elevate Alec Stewart, the regimented, proud but seemingly inflexible south Londoner who had honed his game in Perth? That would give him a marked advantage in some people's estimation, there being a fixation on all things Australian, whether it be their Academy, their climate, their competitiveness or their innate talent. Or should we plump for the younger and more learned Michael Atherton, who had recently established himself in the team?

Ted Dexter was of the same opinion as me that Atherton possessed a better cricketing brain than Stewart. A C Smith, as chief executive of the Test and County Cricket Board, thought much the same and Frank Chamberlain, the then chairman, did not interfere with our choice. We respected Micky Stewart's support for his son, although I hardly expected Dexter to make this public as he did at a press conference to announce our selection. Dexter specialised in public relations but this was an instance of providing the media with more information than should have been divulged. It came across as if Stewart was putting the interests of his son ahead of the greater good.

The first time I came across Atherton was when he made his debut against Essex for Cambridge University in 1987. He was the one batsman to score runs against us, finishing with an unbeaten 73, which especially irritated me as this prolonged the match at Fenner's and I was keen to go fishing. He says I described him as 'an irritating little prick' within earshot, but I cannot recall that. Three years later I got to know him when I coached the England A team in Zimbabwe. He struck me as a determined batsman, lacking the flair of, say, Graham Thorpe. When I first saw Thorpe, at about the age of 15, I could state with certainty that he would play for England; I could not be so sure about Atherton. On that A tour, his leg spin was more noticeably to the fore and he looked more likely to take wickets than anybody else.

What was not in question was his maturity and intelligence. He did not lead that party but he could well have captained England at the age of 21, although he had little experience of leadership, having captained a weak Cambridge team only, but he soon demonstrated the tactical nous that would make him as competent a captain as Nasser Hussain – perhaps a better one when it came to man-management. Atherton could be hard on somebody who stepped out of line but he would not bawl that person out in front of everybody else. He learned to handle Phil Tufnell, who had constant marital problems, especially when away on tour. In Australia, we thought we would have to send Tufnell home because we reckoned that, in spite of eventually surviving India, he had flipped once more.

Atherton handled Phil DeFreitas, who had tried to bully him when they played together for Lancashire, particularly fairly. This was an instance of a senior pro knocking an up-and-coming star, an attitude that stemmed from the days when junior players made the tea and cleaned the boots of the long-serving players and were not encouraged to contribute to dressing-room debate. Lancashire had a few problems in this regard, which no doubt was one reason why they did not win the County Championship for decades.

I could not stand that attitude and, thankfully, it is rarely to be found now – unless, of course, a young lad is talking a load of drivel. If anyone behaved like that in the Essex dressing room he knew he would be in trouble. I always thought of players in the same team as being equals. Unfortunately, after I left to coach England, it seems Neil Foster talked down to the younger players in a condescending and unnecessarily aggressive way. It wouldn't have happened if I'd been there.

When it came to DeFreitas, Atherton could simply have said this was not a selection he wanted and no one would have demurred. It was questionable whether DeFreitas should have been playing anyway. Creditably, he opted to handle him as best he could. Successful captains do not shirk this kind of responsibility and nor should they be denied the awkward personality of their choosing, as was the case in 1974–75 when England did not take John Snow to Australia, contrary to the wishes of Mike Denness.

By the summer of 1993, Atherton had settled into the team to the extent that he scored runs off the high-class opposition that Australia were constantly providing, including an innings of 99 at Lord's. He failed to reach his century only because he slipped and was run out after being sent back by Mike Gatting. Above all, he was gritty and made the most of his ability, which could not be said of some of his colleagues. His career average was fairly similar to mine – just shy of 40, which supposedly is the benchmark dividing good and very good players. Arguably, he would have been a better batsman still had he played in better teams, for this is one way in which a batsman's game tends to improve. I had been fortunate enough to be surrounded by more accomplished cricketers, who, however reluctant they may have been to dispense advice, were nonetheless so technically high-class that I could learn from watching them. There was scant competition for Atherton's place at the top of the order. By now, he was an automatic selection, but the downside was that England were over-dependent on him making a considerable contribution.

In terms of helping him with his technique, I tried to get him to come further forward to the full-length ball to cover the area three to four inches outside off stump that the best bowlers always try to probe. Atherton's tendency was to play too much from leg side of the ball. His head would be three inches away from the correct line. Another failing, if it could be called that because he scored heavily in this way, was that his main run-getting areas were too square on both sides of the wicket. He opened the face of the bat too much. So we worked on him driving the ball straighter, which is not to say we did not work also on his strengths square of the wicket. His game would have diminished if we had not expected him to utilise these shots to the full.

As he grew older, his back trouble, which he never moaned about, prevented him moving fully forward. He went through a tremendous amount of pain and sometimes could not do anything other than lie prostrate in the dressing room when he came off the field. This led to a difficulty in 'sniffing' the ball at the crease, in having his nose over it, in addition to needing constant injections. He especially struggled against Glenn McGrath, whose length and tendency to gain additional bounce troubled all the best batsmen.

Atherton's approach to captaincy was a little more relaxed than Gooch's. He reasoned that England players should be given more time off in between matches, which certainly appealed to Tufnell. The party we took to the Caribbean in the winter of 1993–94 was never likely to beat the West Indies but without Atherton we would have struggled even more than we did at times. He was dogged, brave when facing some highly charged bowling from Courtney Walsh that was obviously intended to undermine the team as a whole, and much deserved the great triumph in Barbados, where Stewart scored two centuries. No visiting Test team had won there for fifty-nine years, which meant it was a terrific achievement, and yet we had to face the fact that this, like the victory at The Oval against Australia in the previous summer, made no difference to the outcome of the series. We lost once more by 3–1.

Our selectorial meeting to choose the party for the Caribbean had begun in curious circumstances. We met not in an hotel, as was customary, but in a room in the pavilion at Lord's that I had not been into before then. It was dark, fusty and rather forbidding. Before anyone had the chance to speak, A.C. Smith, pin-striped suit and all, got down on all fours and searched for bugs. As the diplomatic chief executive of the Test and County Cricket Board, he was paranoid about being quoted on anything; the prospect of having his thoughts recorded by a tabloid newspaper or any other eavesdropper was evidently highly alarming to him and his actions were indicative of an atmosphere fraught with suspicion. Having ascertained no recording devices were concealed about the place, we were able to proceed and pick, in unity, as competent a group of players as was available.

My only previous experience of coaching in the Caribbean had left me somewhat frustrated. The England A party I took there had comprised Test players in the making. The results in the matches we played were of considerably less importance than the knowledge and expertise that would be acquired in such conditions, so I thought it would be worthwhile to go out into the middle to speak to the players during drinks breaks. This occurs at junior county levels and is the kind of thinking that would be second nature to the football manager who calls players over to the touchline. However, the umpires told me to leave the pitch and the West Indies Board of Control would not sanction the idea. I wish the International Cricket Council would do so even now.

I never thought this could apply at Test level and, anyway, in 1993–94 I had more pressing concerns. The difficulty we faced, once again, was that the key members of the opposition were of an altogether higher standing than our best players. Courtney Walsh and Curtly Ambrose were still at their zenith and, as with other West Indian fast bowlers before them, made the essential difference between the teams – them and Brian Lara. We lost the first two Tests by an innings, in spite of Atherton, Robin Smith and Stewart all making high scores, and collapsed humiliatingly in Trinidad in the third of the series when we were dismissed for 46, only one run more than England's lowest total in history. Although I felt shattered at the time, I knew how vital it was to maintain my equilibrium. There was no point lashing out in the aftermath – with whom would I have started? Atherton and I both felt it was best to say nothing at all and try to pick up the pieces the following day. I knew that, however much cajoling I did and however many coaching sessions I implemented, the best players available simply were not good enough. It brought home to me the loneliness and detachment of the job – not being part of a team and in particular not being able to make decisions in the middle when England were in the field. Waiting until the lunch or tea break could often be too late. A decade earlier, Ray Illingworth had come to the same conclusions when, at the age of 50 and unable to dictate the course of events from the dressing room, he appointed himself captain as well as manager of Yorkshire.

Alas, by 1994 I was too old to try returning to first-class cricket, let alone Test matches.

That series in the West Indies is best remembered now for Stewart's two innings on an even-paced pitch in Barbados, Brian Lara's record-breaking 375 in Antigua and the collapse in Trinidad on an uneven surface. What was especially disheartening about that second innings dismissal for 46 was that we had been in sight of victory. At one stage, the West Indies were only 67 runs ahead of us with one recognised batsman left, but as a result of dropped catches, predominantly by Graeme Hick, our safest slip fielder, we allowed them to reach a position where we needed 194 to win. We knew, what was more, that we would have to contend with Walsh and Ambrose bowling unchanged in the final session and then again when they were fresh the following morning.

It is no coincidence that since these two exceptional fast bowlers have retired, West Indies' cricket has slumbered. Their officials complacently thought that more of that ilk would come along, without taking into account the inadequate facilities in all the islands except Barbados, and the lack of good coaching and an Academy. A presumption prevailed that young boys would gravitate towards cricket. They simply did not understand that boys could be lured away to other new-found activities. The American influence was becoming especially apparent and any number of different sports were being introduced at the Garfield Sobers gymnasium in Barbados. The United States appealed to many young West Indians as the land not so much of the free but of countless riches, and basketball appeared to have a particular pull, especially if a scholarship could be won. English football matches, beamed by satellite into bars, highlighted the growing number of black players. Dwight Yorke, of Trinidad and Tobago and the

Premier League, was earning sums that his good friend Brian Lara could not hope to accrue. There was scant money in cricket in the Caribbean. A shortage of sponsorship was reflected in the earnings of the leading players.

In the mid 1990s, Ambrose, Walsh and Lara excelled to the extent that such rumblings could be glossed over for the time being. Our second innings in Port of Spain got off to the worst possible start with Atherton out to Ambrose's first ball and Mark Ramprakash run out off his fifth. Overnight, after just 15 overs following a rain break, we were 40 for eight and did not last much longer next morning. This was perhaps the lowest period of my two and a half years as coach. I could not move from my seat and felt shattered. There were no words to be said. The players were shocked to the extent that they were almost zombie-like. It would have been best if we had gone straight from Trinidad to Barbados, the one island where there were decent practice facilities, but we moved on instead to Grenada, where a strong Board XI made up of players on the fringe of the West Indies team defeated us by eight wickets. In the second innings we collapsed from 140 for one to 165 all out. I could think of only two players who would have motivated themselves in the circumstances for this kind of fixture – Graham Gooch and Allan Border – and neither was available to us, Gooch having decided to stay at home for family reasons and because of the poor practice facilities. With the series already decided, all that was left to play for was personal and professional pride. Fortunately, Atherton and Stewart had lashings of both.

In scoring two centuries in Barbados, Stewart enhanced his standing in the game and amply demonstrated what a fine player he was of quick bowling, particularly on a pitch with such consistently even bounce that he could hook and pull with impunity. I liked him as a person. He maintained high standards and never gave me a moment's trouble, as expected considering who his father was. Robin Smith, by contrast, was affected by the uneven surfaces that we came across throughout the Caribbean – that and his love of the good life. He, too, was a likeable individual and I admired his thorough loyalty to Hampshire – he deserved a much more successful benefit than he received – but he could have done with a measure of Stewart's dedication on that tour. Twice he overslept when he was supposed to be at the ground, which could not be excused by his pleasant nature. When I sent Doug Insole to his hotel room to find out where he was, Smith, who was still in bed, invited him in for a cup of tea.

In the final Test of the series in Antigua, Smith did excel. He made 175, an innings that, unfortunately for him, will barely be recalled other than in statistical notes due to the little matter of Lara breaking Garry Sobers' world record of 365 not out. The first thing to say about this was that it was an extremely flat pitch. Ambrose and Walsh bowled 80 overs between them in one innings and took just one wicket. The other point is that, in my opinion, Lara, who followed this in England with the record first-class score of 501 against a poor Durham attack, is an over-rated batsman. He is not in the class of Ricky Ponting, Jacques Kallis or Sachin Tendulkar, to say nothing of Sobers himself, Viv Richards or Gordon Greenidge. In conditions such as those in Antigua he will destroy an attack, but he is less adept on pitches with bounce and pace in them. He is unorthodox and has not eradicated a weakness against the ball above waist height. Ponting is more of an all-round player; Tendulkar is simply better.

At St John's, Sobers strode out to the middle to embrace Lara in what amounted to a publicity stunt and the match came to a complete standstill for what seemed to be an age. Still, you could forgive Sir Garry anything. He was the most generous of individuals in his playing days (less so about some players of the more recent past) and regarded Lara, who averaged nearly 100 in the series and of whom he was clearly fond, as a worthy batsman to beat his record. Praise indeed! The reality, though, is that there is no comparison. Sobers was the finest cricketer I ever saw and probably the greatest ever, at any rate in Test cricket, when he applied his full concentration. I never saw Bradman but I cannot imagine there could ever have been a better batsman than Sobers. He possessed the rare ability to drive through the line of the ball without moving his feet more than was absolutely necessary. He was still to the pitch of the ball but did not lunge at it. In addition to this, he could bowl in three different styles, was as dangerous as just about anyone in the game if he chose to take the new ball ahead of Wes Hall and Charlie Griffith, and was an excellent close-to-the-wicket fieldsman.

When Sobers played for Nottinghamshire, he would have a laugh and a joke with the fielder he passed on his way out to bat and you knew he would be taking things more light-heartedly. He would still smash the bowling around, but he would often be out once he had made 70. Gambling, horse-racing, golf and enjoying a drink and a good time also came into his orbit. He would have been a mega sporting star these days, but then, as even Atherton discovered a couple of decades later, accident of birth determines an awful lot – Hussain prospered more than he did out of playing for England that little bit longer in the age of central contracts.

At the end of the series I spoke to the media about the soft ways of county cricket in England, by which I meant that too many players who were not good enough were earning a living playing cricket. Standards had fallen since the 1970s partly because the *best* overseas cricketers were no longer available all the time on account of greater international commitments, and partly because of the short-term outlook of a number of clubs – what might be called the football mentality. In other words, a lack of tolerance of anything other than instant success was starting to pervade the game and, as I was to discover, Essex in particular. The state of the county game was certainly an immediate concern to English cricket. For me, however, there was a still more pressing matter to deal with – a new chairman of selectors had been appointed and Ray Illingworth had a following wind behind him.

CHAPTER 4

VOTED OUT

In March 1995 I was asked to provide some comments on the state of English cricket for the Test and County Cricket Board development and executive committees. Following the defeat in the West Indies, another tour, this time to Australia, had ended in defeat. These were the observations I made: 'When I ask England batsmen how they intend to play certain bowlers, it is obvious they have no answers. They bat the same way on all pitches and against all types of bowlers. Each batsman should know where he is going to score his runs. He should eliminate the risky shot and play into the safe areas, depending on the conditions and the bowler.

'There is no excuse for poor fielding. Every county can and should practise this skill daily. This does not happen. I know some players are not keen to work on these skills but the counties must take some responsibility. I should not have to teach England players how to field when they reach Test level. They should be fielding to the best of their ability for their counties. I know the counties that practise fielding skills continually by the standard of their players' fielding. Sixty per cent of the touring teams since I have been involved, including the England A sides, have been under-achievers in fielding skills.'

I never discovered to what extent these thoughts were acted upon by the officials who constituted the hierarchy of the TCCB. Dennis Silk, a burly former headmaster and rugby player, had taken over from Frank Chamberlain as the chairman by this point. He was pleasant enough to me but I never knew how supportive of me he was in committee. As someone who was new to cricket administration, his tendency was to travel the way the wind was blowing. A.C. Smith – Alan, but always known within the game by his initials – to whom I reported in his capacity as chief executive, was a person I liked and trusted. I had known him for years. He has not forgotten that, on the famous occasion when he took a hat-trick after discarding his wicket-keeping pads and coming on to bowl for Warwickshire against Essex at Clacton in 1965, I was his third victim. He says that I scooped up a catch to the leg-side field. In fact, he was not a bad medium pacer.

It was only a pity that there were not more of his ilk around. He was no businessman but was ideally suited to the diplomacy that his position required. I also got on well with Tim Lamb, who was then the cricket secretary of the TCCB, but I could foresee some of the difficulties he would experience upon succeeding Smith. He could be obstinate and, if he thought he was in the right, implacable. I would attend meetings with him and Patrick Whittingdale, the City businessman whose firm was at the time one of the main England sponsors, and there would have to be interludes while both men cooled down by walking around Lord's in different directions. When he became chief executive, Lamb was to have an equally difficult relationship with Nasser Hussain.

One of the trickiest aspects of my job was that, although I reported to Smith or Lamb, I was effectively employed by a TCCB committee made up of county chairmen. If they could not attend a meeting, the chief executives were sent along instead. This resulted in political manoeuvring of the kind that I was not accustomed to at Essex – the sort that Doug Insole had warned me about. Ray Illingworth revelled in this when he was seeking heightened power, canvassing chairmen including Sir Lawrence Byford, the policeman from Yorkshire whom he would have known well, and Duncan Fearnley, the bat-maker from Worcestershire. As chairman of selectors, he would have seen plenty of them when he was entertained in committee rooms. To me, it is both sad and ridiculous that cricket administration should dissolve into politicisation. Administrators always seemed to feel they had to be seen to be doing something to justify their positions, or their perks.

I would undertake one or two particular aspects of the job differently, given the chance again. If I had been more hard-nosed, I might have dispensed with Geoff Arnold. He was as competent a bowling coach as there can ever have been but he irritated the TCCB. He was a poor tourist – he suffered from homesickness and hated having to attend cocktail parties and official receptions. (Alan Knott and Geoff Boycott were much the same as players, whereas I enjoyed the food and drink and being able to get out of the hotel. There was usually somebody interesting around to chat to.) Rightly or wrongly, I stuck up for Arnold and possibly the TCCB held that against me. Smith and Lamb indicated as much.

I should definitely have fired Dave Roberts, the England physio, following our tour to India. He had succeeded Laurie Brown, of Manchester United fame, and was known to crick-eters through his official capacity on Ian Botham's charity walks the length of Britain. He loved mixing with celebrities but he was a dreadful self-confessed moaner. I realised this in Pakistan when he wanted to leave the England A tour and go home because he thought we might be caught up in the Gulf War. A coach should not have to look after his physio, as I had to do with him, but when considering getting rid of him, I took into account that he had a family to support. In his end-of-tour report post-Australia, he stated that our preparation before matches had not been rigorous enough with not enough stretching exercises. I allotted him twenty minutes each session, but these would get off to a bad start with Michael Atherton saying, 'Let's get this twenty minutes of aimless exercise over with.' Roberts thought Atherton was taking the micky – as he was – and reported back critically to the TCCB. He had a guilty conscience about it and wrote me an apologetic letter, stating that his career would not have progressed 'without my unstinting support' and that his 'stomach churned' when he learned of my fate. Given that I had supported his promotion from England A, evidently he regretted making such critical comments. Doug Insole told me later that his report had not helped my position.

I think when I became England coach I did not appreciate the difference between coaching or leading a group of people in Essex whom I had either grown up with or had known for a very long time, and dealing with some individuals whom I neither knew nor could understand. The camaraderie at Chelmsford was the envy of the county circuit and I was simply not accustomed to coping with complex players who did not necessarily respond to straightforward team talks or tactical suggestions, or, in certain cases, raise their game when representing their country. I have always been happiest in my own environment. Perhaps some England players thought I was stand-offish whereas I am fundamentally a shy person. I found it frustrating that I could not communicate with them as I would have liked or influence the course of a match on the field while I was sitting on the pavilion balcony. Players can use the coach as an excuse for their own poor form and I was aware that there were players, one or two of whom I considered shallow, who were talking to the likes of Illingworth and Fearnley behind my back. A coach's life is a solitary one during the day and, often, in the evening as well. I suspect that is more to Duncan Fletcher's liking than mine but there was never a day when I thought that I should have stayed with Essex and not taken on the job. I simply could not turn down such an offer.

I was not aware that I had alienated any of the players whom I coached. I never got the impression they were rebelling against so-called 'outdated' methods. Our fielding drills, which were quite new then, were similar to those of Australia. By the end of a tour some of these do become slightly boring – high catches and slip catches are the same whenever they are practised. I would tell the players when they hadn't done the right thing or hadn't played well, but I wouldn't hold any grudges, even when some of them were dismissed playing shots that should not have been applicable in the conditions in which they were batting, which was a continual frustration. A cricketer thinking on his feet should know not to try to hit an inswinging bowler through the covers or play against the spin on a turning pitch. The coach of England should not have to teach his players how to play slow bowling. Whatever the level, batsmen were not analysing the game as they had in the past, which may have been because of the extra time spent on physical preparation at the start or end of the day or the lack of time spent in discussion over a drink at close of play, which they were no longer encouraged to do at county level. Perhaps they were attempting to score quickly because that was considered the vogue. Maybe this was a legacy of too much county cricket on bland pitches but I thought that these players should have worked out the percentages – the chances of succeeding – better than they did. When I pointed this out in the dressing room after they were dismissed, they looked at me as if I was mad. I would tell them where they had gone wrong, whether this was over their batting or bowling or why they were drifting off in the field and not appreciating that a particular batsman was trying to farm the strike. What was said was out in the open and, as far as I was concerned, that was the end of the matter. I certainly blew up more as captain than as coach because I was out on the field and did not have to wait until an interval.

Before I left for a skiing holiday in Morzine in the French Alps in March, Smith told me to telephone him on a certain day at a certain time, after a meeting of the TCCB's executive committee, which indicated my position would be under discussion if not review. This was before the days of mobile phones and there was no telephone in my apartment. In the one pay-phone box I found at the top of a ski-lift, a woman was having a seemingly endless conversation. When she eventually came out, it did not occur to me to reverse the charges (or claim the French coins back on expenses as certain Yorkshiremen would have done). I got through to both Smith and Silk. They told me, in an apologetic and sympathetic way, that I was not wanted any more. Silk was to write me a note of commiseration. 'You must feel I have been a treacherous person to allow this to happen. I was disappointed about the lack of progress some of our players were making and felt you were sometimes too kind to them. I am well aware that it won't be all that long before the guillotine descends on my neck and then perhaps we can go off to Ireland and fish together and look with pity on those who have high-profile jobs in cricket,' were his words. In fact, he was to stand down before he got the chop – and we never did visit the Emerald Isle.

Was I too kind? It is true that I was protective of the players, as I would expect any coach to have been of me. I saw no purpose in constantly making public criticisms and do not believe Illingworth's antagonism achieved anything at all. He was fortunate to have a captain in Atherton who did not respond in kind. Certainly I was critical of the players in private – so much so that towards the end of the Australian tour I told them that their jobs were on the line. Ultimately, whatever the coach may say, players have to push themselves if they want to be successful. My belief was that not enough of them had that instinctive desire.

It was my good fortune that I was skiing with David Masson, a friend and experienced businessman who was negotiating a new contract with CarnaudMetalbox. He advised me not to resign as I had nearly three years of my contract still to run and could negotiate a settlement so long as we made it clear that I had been sacked. In due course, the TCCB was very fair about paying me for the remaining period of my contract, although, given the demands on my time, I do not think in retrospect I was properly paid over my two and a half years. I carried on skiing with my wife and friends for another week and it amused me that a few journalists came out to the slopes in an attempt to interview me, even though they had no idea in which resort I was staying. Spotting members of your own family in the middle of a piste when they are all wearing goggles, hats and ski clothes is hard enough, so I was not surprised that I couldn't be found.

The voting was seemingly clear-cut, even though that had not always been the case at TCCB meetings of old. When Silk was elected chairman, Mike Vockins, the chief executive of Worcestershire, marked his cross in the wrong place – he had meant to put it against the name of Silk's chief rival, Ossie Wheatley. Somehow, Dennis Amiss, my old friend from our touring days, managed to vote for Brian Bolus rather than himself for a place on the England management committee. Bolus was a loose canon who could not keep anything to himself when he was a selector. He liked the kudos of being associated with England so that he could increase his fees for after-dinner speaking.

I was to learn that David Acfield, in his capacity as chairman of the cricket committee, had been the only person to favour my retention at the TCCB executive committee meeting in question. Smith was supportive but, although he had a vote, he did not exercise it as he soon realised a majority of the nine voting members wanted to make a change. Acfield had been deliberately kept out of any previous relevant discussions and his relationship with Illingworth, which had been a pretty friendly one hitherto on account of their both being off-spinners, has not been the same since. Illingworth, who apparently spoke quite fairly but through whom the disaffection of players was channelled, was all too aware that Acfield would support me. Doug Insole, who had a vote over my future in his capacity as chairman of the international committee, abstained. Mike Smith, my tour manager, did not have a vote. Byford and Fearnley advocated change on the basis of poor results and the players, as a whole, did not give me their backing. I was subsequently told that they had lost confidence and it would not be easy to restore it. This counted against me more than the bad defeats for there was a general realisation that the team was not good enough. The fact that I had been given a long contract stuck in the craw of some executive committee members – even Insole felt that had not been good business policy.

All in all, the conclusion of the meeting was that it was time for a change and I could not dispute that results were indifferent. Even so, I gave the job everything I could, seemingly for twenty-four hours a day on tour, wet-nursing the players and having to be a parent to most of them, who were homesick. The idea that touring is fun is an illusion. In reality it consists of hotels (some of them nice, some indifferent; in my playing days in India, we found rats in rooms), airports and cricket grounds. In the age of one-day series, day/night matches and compact tours, albeit more of them, there is not the time for a leisurely look round the Empire of old. I would have enjoyed the more relaxed trips of the past, not least because such places as Georgetown and Kingston would not have been the dumps they are today.

As for the media, I think journalists were reasonably fair to me, although I eventually refused to give any more sound-bites to Radio Four since the questions came in along the lines of, 'Don't you think it's time you should resign?' I recall being upset on just one other occasion, when Simon Hughes in his capacity as player turned pundit said we had not studied Shane Warne properly. We had.

The correspondents I knew well and trusted from my playing days, such as John Woodcock and Michael Melford, had retired, but I did not dislike their successors. I never attended any media training course, which is a worthwhile exercise for players today, but I quite enjoyed press conferences, working out in advance what the questions would be, and cared only that articles were factually accurate. Even when the *Sun* stupidly printed the fax number of our hotel in Australia and invited readers to send their thoughts to me, only one or two unpleasant ones arrived and I passed them on to the police. Some were quite humorous. For every crank, there was a supportive note, including one from that well-known purchaser of tabloids, Micky Stewart. Any suspicious parcels I received around this time I gave to Alan Lilley, my old Essex colleague, who had the bravado appropriate for a son of a policeman. He is still with us, so there cannot have been any explosives.

The role taken on by Duncan Fletcher, with whom I am often confused, has become wholly different from the one I undertook. Quite apart from having the use of the National Academy at Loughborough, he has a plethora of assistants. I had to arrange fitness sessions at Lilleshall, ensuring the right trainers were hired, whereas he has somebody to organise that. Before our tour of India, I had to unearth the right sort of matting to simulate batting against spin. No media spokesman travelled with the team to ensure that the players wore the right sponsors' caps and tracksuits before being photographed, or indeed to bring the right player to a press conference. I was there at close of play for the first four days of every Test. As for trying to make Atherton, Hussain, Graham Thorpe or even Gooch wear the proper item of clothing, it was almost impossible. All of this meant not much time remained for what I was actually supposed to be doing, namely trying to improve the techniques of individuals who were not performing at the requisite level for Test cricket.

Perhaps the most significant way in which Duncan Fletcher has benefited has been over the introduction of central contracts in 2000, whereby the best players in England are under the control of the head coach. David Lloyd and Atherton had pressed the England and Wales Cricket Board (as the Test and County Cricket Board had become by then) for this change and Fletcher has been the one for whom it has been a boon. If the chairmen of all the county clubs could have agreed a clear policy over when to rest their leading players, the implementation of central contracts would not have been necessary but the counties tended to look after themselves and, inevitably, wanted the stars to turn out for them. I can understand this – when I was captain of Essex, I wanted Graham Gooch and Neil Foster in my team, and they wanted to be in it as well.

Otherwise, I had, and have, no quarrel with central contracts. Bowlers require more rest than batsmen, Hussain and Atherton being the exceptions. Batting was harder work for the highly strung Hussain than it was for Gooch and me, so he was right to retire when he did. Atherton's back trouble was such that he would have been a better performer for the rest and, anyway, he was not stimulated by county cricket. As he himself empha-sises, he played three times as many first-class matches as some of the leading Australian batsmen of his era and cannot remember the details of many fixtures, other than the Tests, with much clarity.

There was no concept of central contracts in the early 1990s. I believed then, as I do now, that county cricket provided the right training for Test matches and that my successors should still watch it when they are free of international commit-ments, but the extra time available for preparation now is invaluable. When I was coach, players turned up from all over the country on a Tuesday, had a net in the afternoon, a team dinner on Wednesday evening and were performing the following day. Sometimes they hardly knew their colleagues, as had been the case when I made my debut for England. It was far from an ideal scenario.

When my contract was terminated, although I had enjoyed the challenge, I cannot say I missed every aspect of the role. At the end of a tour, it was a relief to go home and escape the incessant demands from the players and the press. Illingworth took over as team manager and chairman of selectors, drew the series against the West Indies in 1995 and lost by 1–0 in South Africa the following winter. It was soon apparent that he could not combine both roles, as was evidenced when England went out of the World Cup in India and Pakistan at the quarter-finals stage to Sri Lanka. Our preparation for one-day international cricket, which had assumed growing importance, was inadequate. Atherton and I had long known the two positions could not be combined satisfactorily and, a year after my dismissal, Illingworth relinquished the coaching and management side of his position. The TCCB discontinued the post of team manager and appointed David Lloyd, a nice, amusing, slightly mad man – as was shown when he blew his top in Zimbabwe – and an adequate coach, as his successor. He was to last until the end of the 1999 World Cup, with mixed results, until the appointment of Duncan Fletcher.

The TCCB would have known Lloyd was volatile and likely to explode in the heat of the moment. He should have had a tour manager with more experience than John Barclay possessed for England's visit to Zimbabwe in 1996–97. Barclay was too close to the players and not able to guide Lloyd over what to say before he went into a press conference. On every overseas trip, someone who can see the bigger picture is invaluable – someone like Bob Bennett or M.J.K. Smith rather than Phil Neale, whose job is to take care of administrative requirements such as paying bills and booking opera tickets. When things go wrong, a measured opinion is required from a manager who has the authority to move players from a poor hotel, for example. The home authority, if allowed to dictate schedules and itineraries and save money, will not mind making touring uncomfortable for their opponents – and that goes for Cricket Australia as much as anybody else.

The England players thought Lloyd brought enthusiasm and humour to the dressing room, which doubtless he did in his zany way. He would drape union jacks around the lockers and play tapes of Churchill's speeches – not that this appealed to players such as Mark Ramprakash. Cricket is too long a game for that kind of psychology and modern-day players have to be pampered. They want more attention. Lloyd would give of his time but his temper was sometimes simmering.

The ideal coach might have been a combination of elements of him and of me. To an older coach, practising batting, bowling and fielding was by far the most important contribution that could be made. Videoing and analysing technique was just starting to happen and Lloyd was more convinced about its relevance than I was. I do believe this has its place, but to analyse all aspects of the game too deeply is not the ideal approach. Modern-day players all watch themselves on video. They want to be told they are going about their game correctly and not be presented with negative points. Coaches may feel they have to justify their jobs and sometimes over-emphasise technical points. Sometimes they are simply wrong in what they are saying.

I think I was the first person to organise fielding drills at England practices and I insisted on all the team having net practice – including batting practice for those who did not feel they should have to bother about it. Alec Stewart and I disagreed with the prevailing feeling that bowlers should not bother about having a bat in the nets. Some bowlers thought batting and fielding did not come into their game, Devon Malcolm for instance, but we tried to change that view. Yet however much tutoring went on, we could not change certain habits when players went to the middle. Most of them refused to admit to making a mistake when they were dismissed. Australian batsmen did. Usually it was the more insecure players who would not acknowledge that they had made an error at the crease. They were the ones who tended to excel in practice more often than at the wicket – players who bat in the knowledge that, if they err, they have another life and another after that. I've seen a lot of good players in the nets. Ramprakash, alas, is the obvious example of not translating that ability into success in the middle.

It would have been better if Lloyd had taken over from me, for Illingworth put English cricket back by a good two years through not understanding the modern-day player. When Lloyd gave up, Bob Woolmer, whose judgement of a player I rate as highly as anyone's, became the first choice as his successor. I had to be careful whose opinions I took when England coach as everybody would push their own players, but his were valid. Unfortunately but understandably, he wanted a break after coaching South Africa. Negotiations between his agent and Tim Lamb broke down, whereupon a short-list comprising Duncan Fletcher, Dav Whatmore, who was then coaching Sri Lanka, and Jack Birkenshaw was drawn up. Birkenshaw, who had achieved considerable success with an average Leicestershire team, was passed over possibly because he was thought to be in Illingworth's mould.

Duncan Fletcher, the former captain of Zimbabwe and a

man with whom I had had perfunctory dealings when he was coach of Glamorgan, appeared to be a decent enough person, although he said little other than 'good morning', lacked a sense of humour and appeared to have no interest in mixing with opposing coaches. He could be off-hand. He had still less time for administrators, as the governing body would swiftly discover after his appointment. His attitude was markedly anti-establishment (this was to chime with Nasser Hussain) and was reflective of the African *kraal* mentality – a desire to retain independence and wariness of outsiders. Zimbabweans, as I discovered when I came to know Andy Flower, are inherently serious people; perhaps that is inevitable given the conflicts they have grown up with and the fact that many of them, including numerous cricketers, were forced out of their own country.

Fletcher was fortunate in having a great ally in David Morgan, the chairman of Glamorgan and Lord MacLaurin's successor as chairman of the ECB, which the governing body had become in succession to the TCCB. Morgan had observed Fletcher turn his county into champions, no mean feat given that they were not an outstanding team, and no doubt regarded him as a very competent batting coach – which I believe he is. Morgan must know Fletcher better than any other administrator does and be prepared to put up with him treating the ECB generally as if the people employed by it know nothing about the game.

Fletcher is able to work the fact that there has been so much criticism of the structure of the game and the shortage of talent in county cricket to his own advantage. He benefits every time there is a debate over the merits of the Cricket Reform Group set up by Mike Atherton and Bob Willis to look into what is perceived to have gone wrong, and he is well remunerated – as an England coach should be. However, I have not seen Fletcher at a county match since he took the job – in fact, apart from when he is conducting fielding and practice sessions, he is only to be seen in the England dressing room, and in common with many an overseas coach, he is unlikely to be in favour of his team leaving it at close of play to mix with the opposition in the bar.

Players tend to like people who knock the so-called Establishment and hence they like Fletcher. It is one reason why Hussain gelled with him. Another, and this, of course, was more significant, was that Hussain felt Fletcher to be a good coach, as did Atherton – and a good judge of character, which perhaps was because their views on other people were markedly similar. The Glamorgan connections have remained intact. Although Robert Croft struggled to retain his place after Fletcher became coach – I think perhaps because he was judged to be too much of a stirrer – Matthew Maynard, unexpectedly, was taken on in a coaching role. He liked a drink on my tour to the West Indies and was off to any party going. Talented batsman though he is, I personally would not put him forward as a role model for young cricketers. To be fair to him, though, he has worked for his level III coaching qualifications and evidently reckons that this is what he will do full-time upon retirement as a player.

A coach has to get on with his captain, which Fletcher has ensured he has done, be it Atherton, Hussain or Vaughan. His cold-fish demeanour and the fact that he imparts little to the media has meant that he has stayed, unsmiling, in the background. He has not concerned himself even with attempting to form a friendship with key administrators. David Graveney, John Carr and Rodney Marsh, all important figures at selectorial, administrative and coaching levels, have found

Left: A young England hopeful.

Below: With Sue on our wedding day, 1969. The tie gives away how pleased I was to be a Test cricketer by then.

Bottom: There were some highs against Australia. Ray Illingworth has just taken a catch off Derek Underwood's bowling to dismiss John Inverarity in the match in which England retained the Ashes, at Headingley in 1972. That's me far left.

A. WILKES & SON

JOHN WARBURTON

EMPICS

Top: Lillee and Thomson, the most hostile bowling pair in the game's history. They took us apart in 1974/75. Lillee was certainly the best I've ever seen.

Above: I seemed to turn it on against New Zealand, including my highest Test score – 216 – in 1975. This is the Prudential World Cup match that year. I was named Man of the Match, scoring 131.

Right: 1979. Sue, Tara, Sara and the Benson and Hedges trophy. And a personalised Fred Perry shirt, no less.

Full of hope as England captain, on my way to India in 1981, but it all ended rather dismally.

Fourth Test. Boycott didn't want to play, claiming ill health. He had become the leading run-maker in history so perhaps his mind was on other things. Kapil Dev is celebrating.

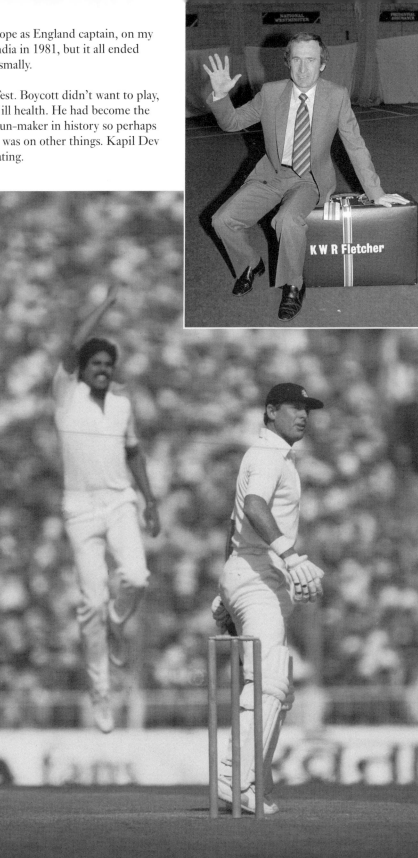

K W R Fletcher

EMPICS

GETTY IMAGES

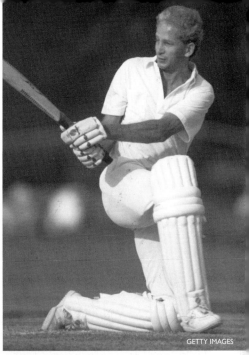

On my appointment as England coach in 1992. Am I trying to indicate how big a task it will be?

Above right: Gower was a fine batsman. I should have insisted on taking him on the 1992/93 tour of India.

Shane Warne's first ball, in the First Test in 1993, announced his arrival in the most dramatic fashion. No one, certainly not Gatting, expected it to turn 2 feet.

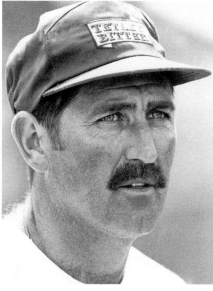

PHILIP BROWN

MIRRORPIX

Above left: Caught unawares at Trent Bridge in 1993, knowing we had thrown away a real chance of winning the Test.

Above: I have the highest regard for Graham Gooch in all respects. The finest cricketer in Essex's history.

MIRRORPIX

Ted Dexter was a conscientious Chairman of Selectors. He resigned in 1993, a few months after this photo, following our Ashes defeat.

1994 Lord's Test against South Africa. The England captain faces the media after appearing to rub a substance on the ball. Atherton and I explained to the officials there was nothing in it. Ray Illingworth (*right, with Michael Atherton*) saw the incident rather differently.

1995. Skiing in France, just before my pre-arranged call to hear my fate as England coach. It wasn't good news.

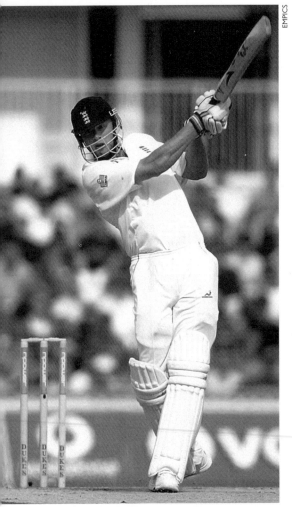

Above: Still very much in the game and in disguise, checking out the opposition for Essex.

Left: Andrew Flintoff – the player England will be primarily dependent on for several years. He looks like a hero and strikes the ball like one.

Below: Both myself and Ray Illingworth should have noticed Michael Vaughan's potential at Test level much earlier.

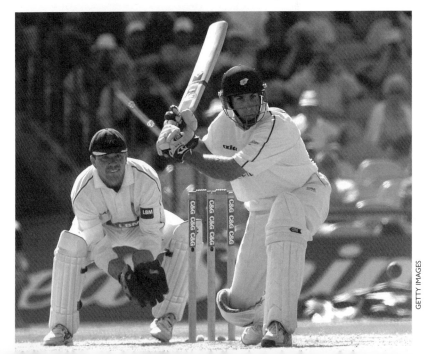

it difficult to work with him. Doug Insole, who has done more unpaid work for English cricket than anyone, asked him one day why Jason Brown, the Northamptonshire off-spinner, was not making the progress expected of him in the game. 'I didn't know he couldn't bat, bowl or field,' was the curt response from Fletcher, who kept walking on as he gave it. There are administrators who would not be too dismayed if he left, for all his success, but they acknowledge that he, not they, will be choosing the moment of his departure.

I'm sure Hussain, Atherton and others have made their thoughts about Duncan Fletcher known to the ECB's management board, acknowledging, I suspect, the fact that he emphasises strengths and weaknesses; can assess a player quickly and accurately; is, as they see it, a sound judge of character; and is not one for criticising his players in public. He saw Steve Harmison's potential and was prepared to allow him time to develop it. He is clearly in his element as a batting coach, as opposed to dispensing advice on wicket-keeping, for example, a task he should have passed on to a specialist such as Alan Knott or Jack Russell earlier than he did. He has enhanced the skills of the best players and, for so long as that is seen to be productive, he will be shielded from sniping.

CHAPTER 5

ILLINGWORTH AND ME

If there was one player with whom my career was inextricably linked, it was Raymond Illingworth. He took my wicket in the second first-class match in which I played, in 1962, and he did what he could to dismiss me in a different sense three decades later when he wanted supreme control over the management and coaching of the England team. In the intervening years, I played with him when I made my Test debut – he bowled Australia out in their second innings through taking six wickets – when we won the Ashes in 1970–71, and in the last Test of his career in 1973, as well as on countless occasions in county cricket. Even now, he still greets me like an old colleague, an old friend, when he sees me. I came to realise that the scheming that went into his own elevation in the game is merely an attitude of mind in Yorkshire. He probably did not imagine that he had treated me in a way that was out of the ordinary because it wasn't in his own county.

The Yorkshire players of his day were often bickering among themselves. The back-biting was such that when something went wrong, it was always someone else's fault. They could not stop picking each other to bits. One of my earliest experiences in the game was of Fred Trueman running naked through the Essex dressing room at Bradford to escape an enraged Brian Close. Yet once out of the pavilion they were united and they always knew how to win. They swiftly worked out what constituted a good score and how they should bowl out the opposition. Gordon Barker, a Yorkshireman brought up in that era who came to play for Essex, was of the same mindset. I learned a tremendous amount just by watching the Yorkshire team, which was highly beneficial when I became captain of Essex. I admired the fact that they planned to win a match from the first ball, not on the second day or on the last afternoon through a run chase.

Illy, as he was known throughout the game, was an excellent county cricketer without managing to establish himself properly as a Test player before he became captain of England in 1969. He had to compete with Fred Titmus and David Allen, both of whom were fine off-spinners, but he was the best batsman of the three and statistically should have done better. Unquestionably, he knew the game. In the conditions he was accustomed to in the north, crumbling turners and wet pitches, he bowled opponents out. He was the type of spinner who needed to bowl with less pace on the ball in order to drop it on to a length on bouncy pitches, unlike, for example, Bishen Bedi, who would flight the ball more. The difficulty was that, like all spinners, he had developed a natural speed; had he been brought up in India, he too would have flighted the ball more. Illingworth was accurate, niggardly, had an arm ball and gained sufficient turn to beat the bat. On flat pitches he protected his own bowling figures, preferring to come on just before lunch and then in late afternoon while the other spinner was left to try to contain batsmen aiming to dominate the attack. His batting, which was technically sound, thrived with the responsibility of captaincy. Overall, his cricket reflected his parsimonious approach to life. I always had a high regard for him as cricketer and captain – no one could have doubted his knowledge of the game, or his shrewdness – but we were never chummy.

When we did have a drink together, he was very pleasant and informative, but I didn't know what was going on behind my back. The machinations of the game were not at all novel to him by the time he had reached the peak of his career in winning the Ashes in Australia. His suspicion of Colin Cowdrey, from whom he had taken over as captain through default, and who was his vice-captain on that 1970–71 tour, was such that he always felt he was being stabbed in the back. The mutual antipathy between them went back to another tour of Australia, in 1962–63, when they had a disagreement over net practice. Illingworth would not have liked Cowdrey having more money than him; Cowdrey, for his part, distanced himself from Illingworth's more professional and money-conscious approach to the game. Unhealthy factions developed as a consequence.

By the time Illingworth sought the role of chairman of selectors in 1994, having been denied it in 1986, he was well conversant with the black arts. His rival for this position was M.J.K. Smith, a man who would have been much more to my liking and who, like Ted Dexter, the out-going chairman, and Colin Cowdrey, disliked Illingworth. Illingworth, for his part, appeared to resent the backgrounds of all three. He felt the game, and life generally, had dealt them a better hand and that his own achievements in county cricket merited more appearances for England; and all three were former England captains who had been responsible for not selecting him at various stages of his career. One reason for this was that Titmus was easier to get on with and was as good a bowler; another was that Allen bowled with more loop and bounce and hence was more valuable on the harder pitches to be found overseas.

In 1993, Illingworth had spotted a way of taking over as chairman through knowing Sir Lawrence Byford, the chairman of Yorkshire, and others on the TCCB committee. He lobbied those whom he felt would be sympathetic, made full use of the media and worked to his own advantage any antipathy towards Oxbridge as represented by Dexter and Smith. While we were losing in Australia, he even suggested in interviews that he should replace me as coach, seeing nothing wrong in such behaviour, which incensed Smith, our manager. Whether or not the TCCB wanted to make a change from the kind of personality that Dexter and Smith represented, I am not sure, but from the moment that Illingworth was appointed chairman of selectors, having established that he would have the final say in selection ahead of me and the captain, I knew just how difficult working with him would be. Had Smith been elected in his place, my own position would have been strengthened and my five years as coach might well have run their course.

What became of particular concern was the manner in which Illingworth tried to distance himself from anything that went wrong. Dexter, however flawed some of his thinking had been, was far more positive and would take more responsibility for selections that had been made. Illingworth, on the other hand, would ensure the press learned what had happened at meetings in which decisions were taken that turned out to be unsuccessful. He would take all the accolades if results or a passage of play went in our favour, and distance himself when things went wrong. I felt it was a poor way to run a selection panel and a team, but he would do it all the time.

Having succeeded Dexter as chairman of selectors, Illingworth initially was responsible only for the selection of the team; later his powers were widened so that he became an overall supremo, as he liked to think of himself. It was clear immediately that he would over-ride my views. Of the defeated team that returned from the West Indies in 1994, only five players were chosen for the First Test that summer against New Zealand – Atherton, Stewart, Smith, Fraser and Hick. He had already been publicly critical of the last two. He also made it clear to Gooch that he would return to the England team only if he made himself available for Australia the following winter. As a further authoritative imprint, Illingworth banned mobile phones and sunglasses and excommunicated Andrew Wingfield Digby, the team's spiritual adviser.

I liked Wingers Diggers, as he was known in the game. He was friendly with Atherton and with John Barclay, for that matter, and went fishing with both. This was an interest that we shared and I had a considerable number of chats with him about the many rivers to which a cricketer can escape around the world. I have never been a church goer or particularly spiritually minded but that did not concern him. The players whom he did assist were chiefly those with a Caribbean background and he was always discreet and sympathetic. The one drawback about his presence, as I saw it, was that he was another person coming into the dressing room, which is best kept for the use of the players. Here I was in agreement with Illingworth but there was no reason why Wingfield Digby could not carry on seeing individuals in private elsewhere, or in the hotel where we were staying. He was pretty hurt to be dispensed with, on the (typically Yorkshire) grounds that if England were going to beat the Aussies that winter, it would not be achieved through crying on other people's shoulders.

I agreed that mobile phones should be kept out of the dressing room – they were a distinct distraction, not least when players were involved in commercial deals – but doing away with sunglasses was totally unnecessary, even if they did look silly perched on a fielder's head. There were, by now, health grounds for allowing players to use them and I could remember occasions abroad when dust and glare would leave your eyes stinging by the close of play. Inevitably, this ban did not last for long.

As well as these decrees, Illingworth ensured that by having the final say in the composition of the team, Craig White, a Yorkshireman whom I knew from my time as England A team coach, would be included for the First Test. I did not disagree with the sentiment. He had a rhythmical action, control and could bat. Unfortunately, he did not possess a strong enough body to contend with day-in, day-out cricket, which he had to undertake before central contracts were introduced. Still, he took the important wicket of Martin Crowe on his debut. We beat New Zealand by an innings and Gooch, who had opted out of going to the Caribbean the previous winter, made a double century. Illingworth was given substantial credit. He spent much of this and subsequent matches in the dressing room rather than the committee room, so it was difficult to escape him and his bidding. The Second and Third Tests were drawn, which meant that England had achieved their first victory in a series at home since 1990. An achievement, certainly, but the opposition was struggling in this post-Richard Hadlee era and there was no doubting that South

Africa, who were coming next, would be an altogether harder proposition.

I believe Illingworth saw the position of chairman of selectors as only a temporary one and a good opportunity to see other parts of the world. It seemed to me that he treated the role as a means of obtaining a free holiday. When he came to Australia in 1994–95, he didn't watch the matches we played in Brisbane, preferring to stay in Sydney and go up the coast. All the while he was making criticisms whenever he saw fit.

I had no say in the choice of his fellow selectors, who, naturally enough because he put their names forward, tended not to disagree with him. Brian Bolus, a Yorkshireman who spent most of his career with Nottinghamshire, was a garrulous individual who could not keep quiet in committee rooms and press boxes – possibly without even realising what he was saying. Becoming a selector ensured he was in the public eye and hence his worth as an after-dinner speaker (at which he excelled) was that much greater. Whatever Illingworth's viewpoint was, he took it up. In addition, he did not want Atherton to be captain and criticised him even after he had scored a century and we had won comfortably in the First Test against New Zealand, which jarred. Fred Titmus, whom I had toured with, I liked and he was harmless. He watched matches and gave his opinions on what he had seen, which were sound enough, but he was not sufficiently forthright and was a bit deaf, which was a drawback in selection meetings. He was not above poking fun at himself over this.

Perhaps the most bizarre incident in Illingworth's time was the ball-tampering affair of 1994 in the Lord's Test against South Africa. It is hard now to convey the gravity of the situation. Two years earlier, there had been dark mutterings over the methods that Waqar Younis and Wasim Akram, the

Pakistan bowlers, used to achieve reverse swing at considerable pace, and this was followed by Imran Khan, their former captain, admitting to having used a bottle top to alter the condition of the ball. Reverse swing was achieved through making one side of the ball damp and smooth and leaving the other side worn, as if it were suede. At that time, we did not have bowlers who could move the ball in such a way. Darren Gough and White were young then. On their home ground of Headingley, where they played for Yorkshire, and at Cardiff and Manchester, although those grounds were often too wet, the pitches were sufficiently rough for the ball to be jagged on one side, but they could not turn this to their advantage.

Picking the seam went on during my career, especially by fast bowlers, but ball-tampering then had more to do with the use of Brylcreem as a form of polish. When Bob Massie, the Australian medium pacer, was making the ball swing to such an inordinate extent in the Lord's Test of 1972, I remember a discussion in the nets about experimenting with lip ice. This was to enable Basil D'Oliveira to impart more swing than he was customarily able to do, but if he did ever try this in the middle, his figures suggested that it did not work. In one-day cricket today, a different, totally legal form of ball-tampering goes on. The quicker the fielders can make the white ball softer, the better, so they throw it in to the wicket-keeper with several bounces to soften it. When hard, the white ball pings off the ground like a golf ball. Now, match referees and umpires check the ball much more regularly and that, plus the presence of TV cameras, means players are reluctant to try anything beyond sucking mints so as to produce more saliva to shine the surface.

In the Lord's Test of 1994, the first Test between England and South Africa for twenty-nine years and hence one attracting world-wide attention, the television cameras picked up the England captain appearing to rub a substance on to the ball before returning it to the bowler from his fielding position. Atherton and I succeeded in convincing the umpires and Peter Burge, the match referee, that this had not been in order to alter the state of the ball by rubbing dirt on to it from the pocket of his flannels. When Atherton bowled his leg-spin on the England A tour of Zimbabwe, he would keep his fingers dry by using dust. More notable spin bowlers, such as Shane Warne and Phil Edmonds, would often wipe sweat off their fingers by rubbing their hands on the crease as they returned to their mark. I could not see how dirt, or dust, would make that much difference to the surface of the ball. Tennis players would keep sawdust in the pockets of their shorts in the old days.

Dirt, dust or sawdust would not have assisted reverse swing. If a bottle top or an instrument to disfigure the ball had been brought out to the middle, that would have been different. Anyone inclined to try it now would be mad to do so, given the focus of umpires, match referees and television cameras. The whole team has to be in the know if there is going to be some interference with the state of the ball, and that was certainly not the case at Lord's. Besides, as a batsman, I never objected to anyone ball-tampering. It was accepted practice to the extent that, when I was captaining Essex on one occasion in a match umpired by the irrepressible Bill Alley, he called me over and told me Stuart Turner was not making much of a fist of picking a seam. He then gave us a demonstration of how to do it.

In my opinion, Illingworth saw this saga as a way to emphasise the fact that he was chairman of selectors and in charge. His decision to inflict a fine of £2000, half for using dirt in his pocket and half for lying about it to Burge, was a way of emphasising his authority as well as being a means to punish the captain. At the time, I just could not understand why he did it. He explained that it was in the interests of the game.

That said, it was a silly thing for an England captain to have done. I was unaware at the time that Atherton had panicked initially in front of Burge, a formidable, headmasterly figure, and told him there had been nothing in his pocket at all. Fortunately, he was resilient enough not to let the criticism from the media affect him. An awful lot of guff was talked, not least by Jonathan Agnew, who became righteous on radio. If he never tampered with the ball during his career with Leicestershire and England, one of his team-mates would have done, for sure.

At least this overshadowed our disastrous performance during the match, which we lost by 356 runs. No doubt all the ballyhoo affected the team. Not one performance of any conviction was forthcoming save for Darren Gough taking four wickets in South Africa's first innings. We were dismissed for 99 in our second innings, bringing the match to a premature end and affording too many people too much time to grumble about Atherton. I remained supportive of him, in public and private, although one of the selectors – Bolus – was not. It was far from a sackable offence and fortunately A.C. Smith and other officials at Lord's thought the same as me.

All this gave Illingworth the impetus he desired to achieve his goal of overall control of the England team in selection and coaching. Atherton found it very difficult to deal with a chairman of selectors who was nice enough to him face to face but not trustworthy. Every so often, snippets of quotes would reach us abroad undermining our positions. M.J.K. Smith, as tour manager in Australia in 1994–95, would challenge

Illingworth on his comments and ask him why he was not supportive of me. Illingworth, for his part, would of course deny the comments and claim he had been misquoted. The same would happen when Atherton and I tackled him. The press, several of whom I knew well, insisted his comments were accurately reported. I soon knew whom to believe.

Atherton retained the captaincy for the Second Test and emphasised his resilience by scoring 99 on the first day of what was to be a rare drawn match at Headingley. That summer, the South Africans were led by Kepler Wessels, a dour Afrikaner who stuck to the basic tenets of captaincy. By contrast, Hansie Cronje, who was to succeed him, seemed too nice. He was friendly enough but appeared to be farming an image, which, as we were to discover, did not reflect his real self. Later, when he played county cricket for Leicestershire and bought Big Macs in the evening in order to save his meal allowance, Essex achieved a fluky victory over them at Chelmsford. Cronje's reaction to this defeat, congratulating every Essex player on the pavilion steps as if they had won the Ashes, was over the top, as if he was trying to cultivate the belief in fair play that he propounded in the infamous Test against England at Centurion in 1999. I had no notion at the time, though, of his darker side.

To us then, he, like Wessels, was a batsman whose wicket was prized. They were not players of the very highest class but individuals, nonetheless, whom we had to extricate from the crease. That did not occur until the third and last Test of the series when Devon Malcolm, in a spell that was simply freakish, did exactly that. I would not have backed him to bowl South Africa out, but at The Oval everything gelled against opponents who did not relish playing anyone above fast medium. Not too many of their batsmen stuck it out and they did not play Darren Gough well, either. The story goes, even though it is now thought to be apocryphal, that when Malcolm was struck on the helmet by Fanie de Villiers in England's second innings, he told the slip cordon that 'you guys are history'. If he did, the significance of the remark passed me by. I did not have the impression that Malcolm looked any more worked up than normal. I had not seen any similar reaction in Jamaica the previous winter when Courtney Walsh tried to hit and injure him and hence prevent him from bowling at us. What was indisputable was that he bowled as he had never bowled before. Malcolm deserves only credit for taking nine wickets for 57 in South Africa's second innings and enabling us to draw the series.

Illingworth did not have a high opinion of Malcolm, and he was not alone in that, but then he did not understand the modern player. He had found managing a county team diffi-cult enough. In the same way that Alec Bedser would hark back to the 1930s and 1940s, Illingworth was living in the 1950s and 1960s. His outlook was that of an old-fashioned Yorkshireman who was not accustomed to the questioning of younger players, whereas I encouraged them to contribute, both with Essex and England. I did not want downtrodden players.

Illingworth was also out of touch with the way in which the game had evolved in Australia, which was worrying since we were touring there that winter. Atherton, on the other hand, knew what it would be like to take a team that included such older, less athletic players as Mike Gatting, whom Illingworth wanted. They would struggle in the field. Illingworth's judge-ment over Martin McCague, whom he thought would bowl fast in Australia, was also suspect. McCague did not have the personality to cope with the criticism he would receive on returning to the country where he had learned to play the game – 'the rat who joined the sinking ship' as one Australian newspaper unkindly dubbed him – or the inclination to undertake the hard work of quick bowling.

When Illingworth came out on tour, he behaved as if there was nothing awry with our relationship. He and his wife, Shirley, whom Sue and I had known for years, were often left on their own and we would take pity on them. He was too old for the dual role when he took it on, his experience of one-day cricket was limited and the World Cup of 1996 was a shambles. The game had moved on since Illingworth played in Australia at an advanced age in 1970–71 and he had not moved with it, which was ultimately to the detriment of English cricket. After the tour of Australia in 1994–95, even when I lost my job, he said something to the media along the lines of me doing my best, but he never contacted me. I did not see him for at least two years and then only by chance during a county fixture at Headingley. He greeted me as if nothing had occurred to affect our relationship – whatever he perceived that to be.

CHAPTER 6

CAPTAINCY

Whether I was leading my county or country, I never found the various facets of captaincy difficult to handle. I was 29 when I was appointed captain of Essex and had been making tactical suggestions and decisions for Brian 'Tonker' Taylor for some while, in much the same way, albeit at a more lowly level of the championship table, that Ray Illingworth and Jimmy Binks had done for Brian Close for Yorkshire. When I led England in 1981–82, I was 37 and possessed quite sufficient experience of Test cricket not to be affected by demands or expectations. I never found any player particularly hard to control, other than Geoffrey Boycott, perhaps, whose idiosyncratic ways I knew well.

Derek Underwood once asked why so many cricketers wanted to captain their teams. It is a good question. So many additional responsibilities can result in an individual losing concentration and focus on his own game. For instance, when I became captain of Essex in 1974, I found I was in great demand as a speaker at cricket clubs within the county. Even though I restricted myself to a couple of dinners a week, these still cut into my time considerably but I agreed because I felt such events were part of my responsibilities as captain. I fell back on some platitudes and such jokes as I knew, but I never enjoyed public speaking. The time could have been put to more profitable use. Addressing a press conference or a dressing room was another matter entirely, and infinitely preferable.

Whether or not this was a contributory factor, I did not make many runs for Essex that first season, when Essex possessed the makings of a decent team. The older players all retired at about the same time and the younger ones were beginning to show that they could take the club on to a higher footing. Taylor was something of a Victorian figure, as smartly turned out as Alec Stewart would always be two decades later, even to the extent that the wicket-keeping gloves he used came straight out of the manufacturer's package. Taylor had been the right captain for us at the right time. He was prepared to play when he had minor ailments, booming his instructions around the grounds, but he possessed a more sensitive nature than most people appreciated. As a wicket-keeper/batsman, he would have fitted comfortably into today's game, for he was a hefty striker of the ball who was ideally suited to opening in one-day cricket. That strikingly stentorian voice was never heard to better effect than on the day when he shouted from the middle at Swansea to David Acfield, our twelfth man, who was in the pavilion perched atop the sixty-seven steps that a batsman had to climb from the boundary edge. Far from cowed, Acfield, who was to become one of my closest friends in the game, kept up a running conversation in his equally booming voice, to the great amusement of the crowd.

Acfield is an intelligent person and a Cambridge Blue. As

well as an off-spinner, he was an Olympic fencer and later a wine merchant and City of London broker. He was one of several emerging bowlers who could be relied upon not to allow the opposition to gain a draw when they were five wickets down. When I became captain of Essex, I could afford to ape Close – who, in spite of his failings, should have captained England for longer – and be aggressive in the field. It would, of course, have been a different matter had I taken on the captaincy ten years earlier. A captain is only as good as the talent around him, although he hopes that his own contribution will enhance it.

I rarely had to enforce disciplinary measures or take a player to one side. On one occasion when I was captaining Essex at Northampton, Ray East, our other spinner, sulked in the field because he did not want to bowl. When it was his turn to bat, he deliberately disobeyed my instructions to play for a draw. I left him out of the next match and, with the backing of the cricket committee, said I would not select him again unless he apologised to the whole team, which he did. The spat lasted three or four days and was over. It was imperative not to hold grudges and, besides, he was a good friend, but in these days of legal action and restraint of trade, I do not think it would be such a straightforward situation, or that committees would be so supportive.

Sometimes I would lose my cool but the moment swiftly passed and we would all be in the bar that night. If I had a go at batsmen for not scoring quickly enough in search of bonus points, I confess the rollockings mainly comprised expletives. I recall coming off the field after one session at Chelmsford in which we had bowled and fielded poorly and shouting at the team, John Lever in particular, that they should have done better. Brian Hughes, the dressing-room attendant, was clearly embarrassed and got up to leave, thinking it was not his place to remain. I told him to sit down and keep quiet, too, because the tea he brewed for us was undrinkable. At this point, needless to say, the whole dressing room cracked up.

The catalyst for the rise of Essex was the introduction of one-day cricket to the domestic game. This began in my first season, 1963, with the Gillette Cup, and by the time I was appointed captain, three trophies were up for grabs, the Sunday League and the Benson & Hedges Cup having been added. I have never been snooty about instant cricket, partly because I have always enjoyed playing it but also because of its appeal to the public. The financial benefits that would accrue for a small and impoverished club such as Essex were immediately apparent. We had the right blend of attacking batsmen, accurate bowlers and, in Keith Boyce, an all-rounder who could have been patented for this form of the game. A certain generation – Yorkshiremen, Colin Cowdrey and a number of cricket correspondents among them – were not so enthusiastic. There was, of course, a danger of overkill and the appeal of the Sunday League was to diminish in the 1990s, but that was far from the case in the first two decades of the competition. I liked the fact that I was freed from conventional cricket in terms of being able to go for my shots come what may, and soon took to the tactical nuances.

A captain's first and, in my view, most important consideration is not to treat everybody the same. Some players need a protective arm placed around them; others benefit from a rollicking. Unfortunately, some captains do tend to regard their teams as extensions of themselves and hence do not differentiate in their approach. Boycott, when he led England for

a brief while, believed that everybody required the same practice and preparation as he did himself, which resulted in
enforced nets on sub-standard pitches abroad and continuing
loss of confidence among batsmen already out of form. Graham
Gooch was of much the same viewpoint, which was far from
accommodating to the two most high-profile players of the
day, Ian Botham and David Gower. When I became England
captain, I reckoned that they knew their best method of preparation for an innings, even if, in Botham's case, that amounted
to huge amusement when he deposited every ball out of the
ground. As the person organising the nets, it was my responsibility to find some more balls – as he knew only too well. I
do not believe I gave Botham too much leeway. The fact that
he went to bed later than others was of no concern to me so
long as he performed properly on the field the next day. He
always wanted to play. Besides, just how much razzing around
is it possible to do in India? Garry Sobers did not go to bed
at all the night before he made a magnificent century in his
last Test appearance at Lord's in 1973. I know how good an
innings it was because I was in the opposition. The difference between Botham and Robin Smith when he favoured
similarly late nights a decade later was that Smith let himself
down in the middle.

I would insist as captain or coach that team practice was
properly adhered to, but if someone preferred to play golf in
the afternoon rather than attend further nets, that was their
prerogative. Most captains I knew were sympathetic to a
player such as Gower, who liked just to check that his timing
was in order, provided – and this is obviously critical – they
performed on the pitch. Botham was certainly of this view,
but he could hardly tell someone not to drink or to go to bed
early when he was not doing that himself. Difficulties in

relationships with the star players would be caused more by a lack of respect, as, for instance, Mike Denness suffered when he led England between 1973 and 1975. Boycott could never understand why he had not been asked to lead the team and there was a general lack of support from the senior players at this time. This was in part because they did not have a regard for Denness as a captain and also, no doubt, because they felt he should not have been in the team in the first place.

My attitude towards captaincy was that, above all, one should be prepared to gamble. I am still irked by the suggestion emanating from my one tour as England captain that I was a defensive captain, which was not the case when I led Essex. I was a great believer in backing my bowlers. I would often leave the opposition what looked on paper to be a fairly easy run chase, but the amount of time we had left ourselves to take their wickets meant that, if we dismissed their first five batsmen, we would reckon on winning. When Essex won the County Championship for the first time in 1979, we did so through bowling out our opponents more often than not. I knew which captains were prepared to give us a game and hence I could negotiate accordingly. It was a different matter when I toured India as England captain, and Sunil Gavaskar, once he had gone ahead in the series, slowed down the over rate as much as he could and drew me into his web.

In county cricket, at least, I could not be accused of being too defensive. I would also gamble on a batsman's ego and arrogance. I recall one particular match against Somerset when they were in their pomp. I reckoned that Viv Richards would not be able to resist trying to strike the ball over midwicket if I brought the fielder in from the boundary. Sure enough, he took the bowler on and smacked a catch straight to Brian Hardie. I have never understood why so many captains place fielders in the deep straight away, pushing mid-off and mid-on back in particular. By all means do so if a batsman hits the ball there repeatedly, but not immediately the bowler has come on. Likewise, Ian Botham would not be able to stand back from that kind of challenge. I always knew that he would try to hit our spinners over the top, particularly on a ground with such small boundaries as Taunton, and I would play on his intentions. I liked to have a fielder close to the bat at short leg – a very brave fielder – as well as a deep square leg. We went on to win that particular match against Somerset and clinched the championship on a turning pitch at Folkestone in the next round of fixtures.

I learned something from all the captains I played under in my formative years. From Trevor Bailey, I appreciated the importance of authority and leadership by example. Taylor, who succeeded him for Essex, was not quite the gruff disciplinarian that he is fondly imagined to be but he emphasised that a team was a unit and that cohesiveness could atone to some extent for a lack of expertise. At the time, the club had just twelve players, so this was indeed necessary. The first-team squad has grown markedly since then, as has the office staff. Micky Stewart, as I have detailed elsewhere, was the best captain I played under, my only regret being that this did not occur in Test matches. At international level, Ray Illingworth was undoubtedly the pick. I never played under Mike Brearley other than on an MCC Under-25 tour of Pakistan in 1967 when we were both still feeling our way in the game, but competed against him often enough to appreciate that he coupled a steely side with the necessary knowledge and a sense of humour. He worked people out well and knew how to manipulate them while always being prepared to back his team. A very good reader of the game, he was prepared to take chances and always had a positive approach with nothing underhand about him. He didn't suffer fools and could become very angry, not least with Phil Edmonds, with whom he never hit it off and always seemed to overcome in an argument. He was the best captain of the modern era.

I disagreed with him – and the others – on occasion. The older and more experienced I became, so the greater the sum of my knowledge, and after ten years in the game I was ready for captaincy. That might sound an obvious statement, but it is far from the case with every cricketer. Some, especially bowlers, were too immersed in their own game to think laterally; others did not think at all. One of the hardest jobs for any leader is to ensure that the concentration of his team is absolute. Fielders would wander out of position; batsmen would not listen to what they were asked to do; bowlers would not adhere to a tactical plan. No wonder captains can be so immersed in their duties that they occasionally slip up. Keith Pont says that once I forgot to tell him he was twelfth man and Essex duly took the field with twelve players. I cannot remember anything about it but he has dined out on that story ever since.

As a young cricketer, I did not think it my place to question a captain's tactics. Only the senior players are kept appraised of plans over, say, the timing of a declaration or whether or not to field upon winning the toss. As captain, I would always encourage the junior members of the team to have their say but a young individual who piped up in such circumstances ran the risk of being branded an upstart. In Australia in 1970–71 I did not agree with Illingworth when he did not enforce the follow-on at Adelaide. They were flat out on their feet. We were 1–0 up in the series but Illingworth was concerned about the impact John Gleeson, the 'mystery bowler' as he was styled, might have on the final day on a wearing pitch if we batted last. Not many of our batsmen could read him, although his googly, bowled out of the front of his hand like that of Jack Iverson and Sonny Ramadhin, was obvious enough. I played him off the pitch by trying to determine which way the ball was spinning, and he did not turn it that much. I sat in the dressing room silently disagreeing with Illingworth but thinking it was not my place to stand up and say so. A match that we could well have won was drawn.

By the time Mike Denness had succeeded him, I was as confident of my place in the team as I ever was and felt I could make a point or two of my own. On the 1973–74 tour of the Caribbean, his first as captain, one of the most inflammatory of all incidents occurred at Port of Spain when Tony Greig threw down Alvin Kallicharran's wicket when he was walking off at close of play. Technically, the batsman was out of his crease, but it was quite evident that he felt, as I did, that the over had ended and hence he was on his way to the pavilion. Denness should have reinstated him straight away but took the view instead that, as the umpire had had no option but to give him out because the ball was not dead, the decision should not be reversed. As we came off, I told Denness that this was quite wrong and that in effect Kallicharran had been cheated out. He had not thought on his feet, as a captain is always required to do. That evening Greig had to be escorted out of the ground by Garry Sobers – no one else would have had the stature to placate such an angry crowd – and I think if the batsman had not been reinstated the next day, the match would have been abandoned.

I disagreed with Denness once again in the First Test of the 1975 series against Australia. Alas, the decision he took that day upon winning the toss and fielding at Edgbaston cost him the England captaincy. He consulted John Edrich, which was fair enough because he was the senior pro, but did not take into account the fact that, as an opening batsman, Edrich's viewpoint could be biased. The pitch appeared green and the chances were that the ball would move around. What happened was that Australia made a convincing total and, as a result of rain, we were caught on a wet pitch. In those days of uncovered pitches, the captain who won the toss was generally advised to bat first. It was particularly necessary to do so in county cricket because matches started on a Saturday and the pitch would be left open to the elements until play resumed on the Monday. The impact that the weather could have was evident in 1974 when we almost beat Pakistan at Lord's – Derek Underwood was the best bowler in the world in damp conditions – and only did not do so because the powers that be in the TCCB panicked and play was called off. This was the beginning of the end for uncovered pitches.

The majority of instances of poor captaincy occurred in one-day cricket when bowlers and fielders had to be shuffled around with proper regard to the conditions as well as the number of remaining overs. Denness was a better captain in this form of the game than in first-class cricket because it was essentially a defensive exercise and the opposition did not have to be bowled out. It was easier to stop them scoring than to dismiss them and hence reading the game assumed less importance. There were set fields and he knew exactly where the fielders should be. In addition to that, he always had the use, for both club and country, of Underwood, bringing him on whenever the opposition was scoring too quickly. The calculations that had to be made suited a metronomic mind.

Other captains responded indifferently. Essex almost won the Benson & Hedges Cup final of 1980 because Jim Watts,

Northamptonshire's captain, took off his slow bowlers, Richard Williams and Peter Willey, and brought back his seamers, Sarfraz Nawaz and Jim Griffiths, on a pitch that was taking spin. We needed 50 runs off the last five overs and Norbert Phillip, our West Indian all-rounder, slogged them to the extent that 30 runs came off two overs from Griffiths. This would have amounted to a diabolical piece of captaincy had we triumphed.

Captains of the day tended to field at first slip or at mid-off, as they often do now, reasoning that those were the best positions from which to keep an eye on the game or the bowler. My preference was for third or fourth slip when the quicker bowlers were on or silly point to the spinners. I was an instinctive catcher of the ball rather than one who followed it from the moment it left the bowler's hand, as you do at first slip, which is effectively akin to a second wicket-keeper. I liked to be in the action, which was not necessarily the case when standing at mid-off. There is always the temptation, too, to say too much to the bowler, as Nasser Hussain appeared to do when he captained England. As for what Geoffrey Boycott would have uttered . . .

Kidology is as much a captain's weapon as a bowler's. Shane Warne chats away to umpires, suggesting that he was close to having the batsman lbw – 'that's not bad, umpire, just missing' – and then having his next appeal upheld even though there is scant difference in where the ball pitched. I liked to keep a close fielder in the batsman's eyeline (a position that Close favoured for himself) to distract him from settling at the crease. I knew not to say anything to Derek Randall when he came in to bat because he liked to have a chat with the fielders. Conversely, if a batsman liked to have no noise about him, I would try to disrupt his concentration. This would not be through saying anything offensive and I did not encourage any of my players to make derogatory comments, as Ian Chappell and Tony Greig did. The worst thing any bowler could do when playing against Gooch was to have a chirp at him. I once saw Steve Malone do that after he had left Essex and gone to play for Hampshire, and Gooch responded with a double century. Malone's new team-mates were not best pleased; they knew exactly what reaction his comments would induce. On another occasion, Eldine Baptiste, playing for Kent, stood pouting in mid-pitch after three successive bouncers had been allowed to go harmlessly by, and this, too, was not wise. Gooch is not often roused to anger but he was then. Never rile the best batsmen is an apt motto.

I came to know a batsman's favoured areas of scoring. I would look at his grip and sense that, if he was bottom-handed, he would collect runs on the leg side of the wicket. A player making his debut against Essex tended not to make too many runs, anyway, but come the next time I played against him, I had a good idea of his capabilities. I did not find it necessary to keep a little book about such habits – they were best stored in my head. After playing for some years against David Steele, who was to take my place with such success against the Australians in 1975, I knew how he liked to get off the mark. He would push his left leg down the pitch, just as he was to do against Dennis Lillee and Jeff Thomson, and try to collect runs through midwicket. In one particular match at Chelmsford, Gooch was making the ball swing away from the bat, so I asked him to give Steele an inswinger first ball and positioned myself at leg slip. Sure enough, Steele attempted a push to the on side but, caught unawares by the change in delivery, tickled it to me.

We managed to dismiss Boycott in similar manner when

facing John Lever, whose natural left-arm slant across the batsman was enhanced by his ability to bring the ball back in to him. Dennis Amiss would on occasion clip the ball into the air four yards or so behind square leg throughout an innings. Tom Graveney, a predominantly front-foot player, would get off the mark through gully. If he had a weakness, it was that he played the ball in front of his pads and thus was not an especially good player of off-spin. So if the pitch was turning, I would bring on an off-break bowler straight away. Colin Cowdrey, like Gooch, had no real weakness other than that they both had a preference for the ball coming on to them above their pads. They found that facing a medium pacer who wobbled the ball about, such as Barry Wood (in Cowdrey's case) or Terry Alderman and Neil Williams (in Gooch's case) was altogether harder work. Cowdrey would have difficulty concentrating. Gooch would have bowled well against himself.

Fielding changes have the additional purpose of making the batsman think about his own game. If he is aware that the opposing captain knows the area in which he might get out, the captain is winning the contest. I regarded such changes of field placings as standard captaincy, information to be stored in the recesses of the brain, although not everybody else did. I was fortunate to have two accurate spinners in David Acfield and Ray East when I was captain of Essex, and one of the greatest of all bowlers in Derek Underwood when I led England, although he was past his peak by then. I could maintain close catchers on turning pitches in the knowledge that they would not bowl what we called 'filth balls'. If two out of six balls in one over spun, that was good enough. Then I could carry on gambling with field placings, taking the responsibility for setting them, albeit in consultation with the bowlers.

Sometimes bowlers would become stroppy if they did not like where I was placing the field for them, but I have always maintained that they need more cosseting than batsmen. John Lever, who delivered more overs than most, appreciated that I was on his side. For several years he, along with Underwood, was the best bowler in the country in county cricket. We could cover for Gooch being away with England, but not Lever; so we were fortunate that he did not play as much Test cricket as he should have done. I always reckoned that the batsman who goes out to the middle on his own to take on an attack, although he has only one life, is essentially playing the game of an individual, whereas bowlers need the support of their team-mates. They have a tendency to be too defensive at times. In most dressing rooms there is a split between the batsmen and the bowlers. If the captain is a batsman, he will tend to side with his openers (or others) who may not be keen to take the first innings in potentially trying conditions if there is the opportunity to field. Edgbaston in 1975 was a clear example of this. I also remember that when Essex dismissed the opposition cheaply, East would sit in the dressing room and say, tongue firmly in cheek, 'The bowlers have done their bit – now it's the batsmen's turn.' Such an attitude, seriously expressed, could do untold harm in other clubs.

That is not to say that there was no stroppiness from batsmen, but generally I could ignore it. I never took any notice of Nasser Hussain's rants. I was, though, taken aback when I asked Boycott to give his opinion of a pitch before a match in India and he replied, 'You're the captain – you go and look at it.' I should, I suppose, have realised that this was the kind of response I was likely to get. For all that, I wanted him in my team.

My appointment as England captain for the tour to India

in 1981–82 should have been the high point of my career. It was recognition of the success I had had with Essex and, I think, the manner in which we brought on young players, as well as reassurance that I could still bat even though I had not played for England for four years. The party included several top-class cricketers. That we lost the series 1–0 had much to do with the age-old problem of contending with the umpiring there – it was the worst I ever came across, so poor that Gooch felt there was no point in his remaining since he was invariably given out when either he had not hit the ball or, in terms of lbw decisions, was not in line. We made an official protest over the umpiring of K.B. Ramaswamy after the First Test in Bombay and he did not stand again in the series, although he reappeared unexpectedly in a one-day international. The standard of the officials inevitably affected the players, but I do not believe my despondency created a wholly negative mindset.

The most important innovation in the game over the past few years, in my view, has been the introduction of neutral officials. Although all umpires were supposed to be neutral, in reality this was not the case. In 1981–82, for instance, Sunil Gavaskar, the Indian captain and a fine accumulator of runs, if not as good a batsman as Boycott, was constantly given the benefit of the doubt, not least when facing Lever. This nullified the contest between new ball and opening batsman and turned it into an unfair one. He got away with too much in his own country.

The tempo of the matches during that series, which were played in differing climates and on the kind of flat pitches that Gavaskar, as a batsman, would have requested, was dispiriting. After India had won the First Test in Bombay, he slowed the over rate down and a good deal of the cricket was unmemorable, which had not been the case on Tony Lewis's tour in 1972–73. Gavaskar may have reckoned that the fewer overs bowled, the less chance of England winning. Even when the spinners were on, 12 overs were bowled an hour instead of 20, as should have been the case. I readily confess that I was not blameless, not least because of the constant hold-ups and distractions, such as mirrors flashed in the batsman's eye, orange peel catapulted on to the ground, policemen walking behind the bowler's arm and the sightscreens never seeming to be in the right place. Although compared to the Indian spinners we fielded bowlers who took some time to complete an over, such as Bob Willis and Graham Dilley, I should not have allowed our over rate to come down to the same tardy level, and I accept that the criticism I received was fair. Unfortunately, if a captain such as Gavaskar can be allowed to make use of this kind of tactic, he will. He was more ambitious for himself than his predecessors, Ajit Wadekar and Bishen Bedi.

I had asked David Brown, an unflagging fast bowler of my generation, whether he would like to come to India in a coaching capacity, chiefly to look after the bowlers, but he was too tied up with his post-cricket career of breeding race-horses. I knew he had a fair knowledge of the game and was aware that bowlers needed helping more than batsmen did. He would have gone down well with the players and, had he been present, he might just have arrested the lethargy and monotony that hung about the series.

In international cricket, the home nation would often prepare an iffy pitch for their opponents in the first match of a series, which is when they are likely to be most vulnerable. Then, as occurred in this series, they tried to protect their lead through extreme caution. Other countries tried other

tactics. Australia's Board of Control would organise our itinerary – which the captain and tour manager had no control
over once it was drawn up – so that early in the tour we would
move from Tasmania, where the climate is similar to that in
Scotland, to the first Test in Brisbane, where the weather is
akin to the tropics. Hence an England team would struggle
to acclimatise to the heat. The difficulty over this was that
well-meaning administrators, such as Donald Carr, Doug
Insole and A.C. Smith, found it hard to believe that other
nations could be so devious.

No system of fines was in place at that time either, so teams
could get away with bowling only eight overs an hour if they
wanted to do so. The pattern of drawn matches was repeating
itself. Insole tried for years to instigate penalties that all countries would have to abide by, but there was scant enthusiasm
from other administrators. Given that the West Indies were
able to rotate four fast bowlers, this was not surprising,
although they should have concerned themselves about
whether or not spectators were receiving value for money. In
India, gates were not affected by the slow over rate because
one-day cricket was not the distraction it is today. Families
would still spend their money on watching Test matches.

I felt frustrated rather than dispirited. My annoyance over
the standard of umpiring, our inability to make any headway
and Gavaskar's tactics came to a head in the Second Test at
Bangalore when I was given out after an appeal for a catch at
the wicket off Ravi Shastri, the left-arm spinner. I knew that
I had not hit the ball. Indeed, of the seven dismissals I suffered
in six weeks in India, I was actually out on just one occasion.
As I left the pitch, I cuffed the bails off with my bat – I could
easily have knocked all three stumps out of the ground. (Boycott
told me afterwards to say that I had just been swatting a fly

away!) Wrong, I know, and I apologised immediately to the President of India's Board of Control. This was the one on-field transgression I made during my career.

The media gave the incident maximum publicity, as was inevitable, and I can only imagine that Peter May, the incoming chairman of selectors, did not think much of it. If there was any one moment when I lost the captaincy, that could have been it. Alec Bedser, I fancy, might have been more understanding. The remaining three Tests were drawn and my contribution with the bat in terms of figures was not sufficiently substantial – anyway, not substantial enough for anyone viewing from afar who did not take into account the difficulties with which we had to contend.

I contented myself at the time with the prospect of India touring England the following summer. On our own pitches, and with seasoned umpires in place, there was no reason to believe that the outcome should not be markedly different. Alas, the legacy of the tour was that several England players had had their fill of touring and no one more so than Boycott. He was of no help to me or to any young batsmen who would have benefited from his advice. Even then, at the tailend of his Test career, he appeared to be concerned about losing his place. To me, his attitude seemed absolutely stupid, but any captain who wished to have a quiet word with him would end up involved in a big row in front of everybody else.

Boycott's prime interest by now was to become the leading run-maker in Test history, even though he had opted out of international cricket for three years in the 1970s, and must have known that his total would be overtaken once he had passed Garry Sobers' 8,032 runs. He managed to do this in the Third Test at Delhi just before Christmas and, in so far as his interest in the tour was concerned, that was it. In the following Test at Calcutta he batted but did not field, claiming to be unwell. That in itself would have been just about acceptable had he given us moral support from the dressing room. Instead, on the last day he went off to play on a local golf course without permission from the management. All in all, he could not come to terms with the country or its food and wanted to go home.

Raman Subba Row, the tour manager, and I tackled him and said the team deserved an apology. At least none of the other players not involved in the match had gone to the golf course with him. A quarter of an hour later he came back to us with a handwritten note stating that he thought he ought to resign and go home. For a player to do this midway through a tour was quite extraordinary but we agreed, providing Boycott apologised to his colleagues, which he did by spearing a note with a fruit knife into a beautiful piece of Indian furniture. It was quite obvious that he did not want to be in India and neither I nor the team wanted him there, either, although initially he did change his mind. The reason given for his going back home was that he had had a spleen operation and this had been affected by his being in India. A further reason was soon apparent. The first breakaway tour of South Africa had been hatched in secrecy and was due to commence a few days after we returned home from India – and Boycott was one of the individuals behind it.

Boycott was proud of his record, rightly so, and of all the runs he had scored, but I cannot avoid wondering whether he ever feels that if he had not been such an aggressive, bristling person, he would have made more friends. He got on with Underwood and Alan Knott, with whom he sometimes roomed, but on a business footing. Later, when he coached certain England players on a freelance basis, he would impart invaluable advice, but his comments on television, which were aimed at the selectors for picking the wrong individuals, as he saw it, could have undermined some young cricketers. Besides, his own technique could be picked to pieces because his trigger movement at the crease took his right foot outside leg stump.

Boycott was completely unconcerned about whom he upset – when he went on television, he saw it as his job to analyse and the batsmen's job to take on board what he said. He didn't mind doing the shooting but didn't want to be shot at. Despite rumours that no one had asked him to become England coach, he would never have taken on the role because, at the time, there was no comparison between what he could earn from that and from his television work. The reason why, quite apart from his unquestioned ability as a batsman, he was the most talked about cricketer of his generation was, I think, because most people were so taken aback by his bluntness. He would make it perfectly clear others were inferior players. 'You don't understand what it's like to be a world-class player,' he would say, and he would mention the expectations of his great Yorkshire public. The crowd at Headingley would stand up when he came into the ground. Personally, I would say he was not as effective as Fred Trueman, whom I didn't particularly like but whom I would put in a higher category, the very highest, of England cricketers.

When I was eventually told about the breakaway tour, on our return to England, I did give careful thought to whether I should join Boycott and Gooch for what would have been, by some way, the best paid month of my life. I was offered £45,000, a fair return even now and a tremendous sum then. Perhaps I was slightly naïve not to ring up Peter May and ask him for an assurance that I would remain captain. After all, as the new chairman of selectors, it was inevitable that he would want to put his imprint on the position. Better still, I should have spoken to Insole, who could have given me a steer to how they were thinking.

I discussed the possibility of taking up the offer with Sue, of course, and with Clem Driver, the Essex scorer and chairman of my benefit committee, and between us we came to the conclusion that, having attained the position of England captain, I should not throw it away lightly. I found out later that if I had gone, Driver would have resigned. It was not that I was intrinsically opposed to playing in or against South Africa. Although I did not like the policy of apartheid, I shared Gooch's belief that sportsmen had no less right to ply their trade in South Africa than businessmen. I wish South Africa had not been excluded from international sport and I am not convinced that it brought about the end of apartheid. Sanctions did. Apart from the fact that the game of cricket was deprived of a fine team, I do not think politics and sport should be mixed. All the white cricketers I knew tried to help in the townships and I found the English-speaking South Africans were generally more friendly to the coloured community than the Afrikaners. These tended to be more interested in rugby than cricket and would have felt the banning of rugby tours far more keenly.

I can honestly say that I knew nothing of the planning of the tour while we were in India, as I told Donald Carr, secretary of the TCCB at the time. I believe that one or two players who went with them signed up just forty-eight hours or so before leaving England. When Boycott asked me in passing during the tour whether I would ever play in South Africa, I replied that I could not envisage doing so while I was still England captain. I regarded it as no more than small talk, although perhaps I should have realised that was not his style. I did not appreciate at the time that when Botham's agent and solicitor flew out to see him, this was not for commercial reasons but to advise him not to sign up, or that meetings were taking place between players who were contemplating joining the trip. Subba Row finds it hard to believe to this day that I was unaware of any clandestine negotiations.

Where I differed with Gooch was over his decision to go to South Africa at all when a long Test career lay ahead of him, whereas for Boycott, John Lever and me, it was a different matter. None of us, as it transpired, played Test cricket again, except when Lever was brought back specifically for one match in 1986. Gooch still felt there had been a vendetta against him by the umpires in India and was unrepentant about his decision to go to South Africa, even when he and the others were banned from Test cricket for three years. As I said then, they knew the score.

I did not expect to be given any kudos from the England selectors for turning down such a lucrative offer, nor any particular praise for our victory in the inaugural Test in Sri Lanka, which followed the tour of India. I was not mistaken; there was none. In fact, there was no contact whatsoever, which concerned me increasingly as the weeks slipped by. I was not made captain of MCC for the traditional opening match of the new season, against the county champions, but Peter May announced that nothing could be read into it. He was a naturally reserved, diplomatic man, so I gave this no detailed thought. Also, as April turned into May, I found my form. If there was any suggestion that, at rising 38, I was no longer capable of maintaining a place as a batsman, a sequence of decent scores should have refuted it.

Besides, the tour of India had not been a disaster. To lose

1–0 on the sub-continent was not exactly unexpected and I felt that, even though I was not likely to be reappointed for the entire summer, I should be granted the initial series against India. No obvious person was available to take over from me, given that Mike Brearley had declared his intention of retiring at the end of the 1982 season and had no wish to be brought back into Test cricket. Ian Botham had lost the position the previous year and would be unlikely to be given another chance so soon. David Gower was still young and, in terms of leadership, inexperienced, and Bob Willis, my vice-captain in India, was reckoned to be too wound up in his own bowling to do more than lead by example. If I was to be jettisoned, I surmised that it would be on cricketing grounds. Allan Lamb had qualified for England and was a better batsman than me, and Derek Randall was in contention as well. I had not made any centuries in the Test matches in India and Sri Lanka and no doubt a view existed that I was expendable. I am certain none of the players undermined me but I could not be so certain about the management.

May finally telephoned me at home a month into the season. When I heard his voice I expected to be told I would be carrying on for the first part of the summer. Instead, he told me, in his precise and measured way, that the selectors had decided to make a change. He did not provide any criticisms or explanation of any sort. He merely thanked me for taking the team to India and said that he would be delighted if I scored so many runs over the coming weeks that they would have no option but to select me. I did score an abundance of runs but he knew as well as I did that my Test career, after fourteen years of uncertainty and insecurity, of hardly knowing from one match to another whether I would be selected, was over. I should, in retrospect, have sought the reasons for my sacking but I was never to meet or talk to May again. I would not have ignored him had we come across each other. Had he lived longer, I would have liked to have discussed with him just why I was no longer wanted. As I understood the matter in subsequent years, this was very much his decision. It was presented to the other selectors by an in-coming chairman who wanted to make a change and they felt obliged to acquiesce.

When I began my career, players were not told individually whether they had been chosen or dropped, but learned of their fate from the radio. Ethics did not seem to matter then and things had hardly changed. May said the press had not yet been notified but it was announced on the radio on the four o'clock bulletin, around the time that he rang me.

When I put the telephone down, I knew I had to be on my own. My two daughters were too young to appreciate what had happened and too chatty to quieten down even if they realised what it meant to me. I left the house and took off in my car in order to be alone, mulling over the reasons behind May's decision. I felt let down because I had been open, honest and frank with them about the approach I had had from South Africa. I wonder now whether May, an amateur in his own time as England captain, would have appreciated the difference such earnings would have made to the life of a professional cricketer. I did not have the prospect of well-paid work in the City of London upon retirement from the game, as he did.

For weeks I could not come to terms with the fact that I was no longer England captain. That weekend I simply could not concentrate on the Benson & Hedges Cup match I was playing at Chelmsford, even though the Essex dressing room was sympathetic and, for once, solemn. Lever, who had done so well in India and knew all too well how hard it had been to bowl out the opposition on such flat pitches, was particularly upset. We collapsed to 14 for six yet somehow still managed to beat Hampshire. I knew, and stated publicly, that if the same instigators of the breakaway tour to South Africa contacted me again, I would take them up, but this was not to be. I not only lost the England captaincy but a large sum of money to boot, although there was no question which I would have preferred to retain.

Essex drifted through that summer. We did not win a trophy, even though I did finish with 1221 runs and contributed significantly in the one-day game. My batting should have been impressive enough, in the course of a normal season, to propel me into Test cricket. If I suffered any lack of enthusiasm for the game, it did not last for long. I did not need to motivate myself to play for Essex because I always relished county cricket and had no intention at that stage of giving up. I was not even thinking in terms of becoming a coach: administration – the running of a club or an indoor school – held more appeal. In addition, I had my second benefit to organise, which meant I was never other than fully stretched or on my own for too long. There was no time in which to fret.

Even so, I apologised to the team before the start of the 1983 season. I admitted I had not been focused on the captaincy and told the players that our cricket would be tightened up now. We were champions again that year and, indeed, the following season. I remained eminently happy as captain of Essex until 1985, when, at my instigation, I stood down in favour of Gooch. His time had come and it was for the good of the club that I made way after twelve seasons, although I continued to assist him as vice-captain and took up the load again in 1987 when he felt the responsibility was affecting his batting. One controversial personal moment occurred during our long run of success and I found myself in trouble with the TCCB. I thought Rodney Ontong, captain of Glamorgan, and I had agreed the terms of a declaration in a championship match that would leave us with a run chase. He reneged on this arrangement – or welshed, to use language that would have caused ill-feeling in Wales. After the match, I told the press that his claims that there had been no target agreed between us were incorrect. I should not have said that he was lying, which I did not appreciate at the time amounted to defamation of character, but that he was not telling the truth. I understood some members of the TCCB's disciplinary committee wanted to ban me for two matches, but ultimately I was given a suspended sentence of two matches.

Between 1982 and 1985 our team was just about the equal of our victorious 1979 XI and won three one-day competitions besides. Allan Border joined us in 1986 and we were champions once more. Our batsmen were still consistent and, as one bowler retired, so another of equal if not superior stature – Neil Foster and Derek Pringle, whose name, but certainly not his cricket, I tended to confuse with Alistair Hignell's – took his place. Remembering people's names has never been my strong point. My own thoughts of playing for England melted away, although, of course, like everybody else in the game, I remained as interested as ever in their progress. I believe – correctly, I hope – that my dismissal was predominantly for cricketing reasons, which, if looked at objectively, were sound enough.

CHAPTER 7

ESSEX COUNTY

I have never visualised Essex as a county of upstarts, commuter towns and dreary roads to tacky seaside resorts. For one thing, I have lived in its more rural communities, firstly at Great Easton and, since 1984, in a little hamlet near Dunmow. This area remains unspoilt – at least until the threatened expansion of Stansted Airport takes place. The church spire of the old wool town of Thaxted is visible when I walk from my home across arable land towards the splendidly named Hangman's Wood and Nick's Hole. I grew up across the border in Cambridgeshire and have played or worked for Essex for more than forty years. The affinity that cricketers of my generation feel with our clubs scarcely seems to exist now. When we won a trophy under my captaincy for the first time in the club's history, the County Championship of 1979, Ray East had tears in his eyes. When asked why he was so emotional, he replied, 'You don't know what it's like to play for Essex.' I regret the lack of loyalty nowadays, brought on in part by an unofficial transfer market as a result of two-divisional cricket. The game has long reflected the workplace and mirrors short-term employment in the wider world. To some players, Essex is just another club or staging post, one that is viewed by businessmen I know as a commodity that can be bought and sold for profit. Chelmsford is a prime central site for possible development, as committee members are well aware.

I was born in Worcester because my parents took refuge with relatives after they had been bombed out of their London home in 1942. They lived in Peckham, so I might have played for Surrey. Had they remained near New Road, I would in all probability have partnered Tom Graveney at the crease on that most delightful of grounds. As it was, my father found work and settled in Cambridgeshire, so Essex was the obvious first-class county for me to join once it was evident that I could progress beyond village cricket. My long association began when one of my teachers, Neville Rumbelow, who appreciated that my future lay not in further education but in sport, wrote to Trevor Bailey suggesting that I should play for the county's young amateurs. I was not academic, but that did not concern me at the time, although it probably would have done had I not shown an aptitude for sport. I regret now that I did not work harder and obtain some qualifications, but then again they would have been of scant assistance to me in the game of cricket.

In common with many secondary schools, there was no organised cricket. Essex, as with other counties, were reliant on teachers to notify them of any boy who would be worth a trial. I was 15 and regarded as having more potential as a leg-spinner than a batsman, just as Nasser Hussain was two decades later. Alas, neither of us was to develop our bowling to the point where we could be considered all-rounders in Test or county cricket. That winter, I was asked to attend coaching in the indoor school at Ilford and the following year, 1960, was taken on to the staff.

By 1962 I was playing for the first team and did not find the game particularly difficult. I always felt I would score runs and hence must have had a lot of self-belief. The fact that I spent just one year in the second XI, which might not have happened had I played for a stronger county, was a help. A young cricketer can spend too much time playing second-team cricket. I always played the ball, not the man. I had not watched first-class cricket other than at Fenner's, Cambridge University's ground, and hence knew little of some opponents who were well-known in the game. In 1963 I made runs against Les Jackson, the Derbyshire fast bowler – the pitch would not have been a particularly good one as it was at Romford – and when I came off, my team-mates told me I had been facing 'a legend'. I could play on all types of pitches because I had been brought up to play on them, so I was able to learn and develop a technique.

In each of my first two seasons I made 1000 runs, but even so was surprised at the speed of my recognition. By 1964, aged 20, I was touted as an England batsman in the making. Essex was then far from the professional county it was to become. Bailey, a fine all-rounder and a man I immediately liked, appeared to run the entire show. There was no such person as a chief executive and no backroom staff such as exists today. Bailey was an outstanding cricketer but lacked the patience to lead what was a poor side culled from an extremely small staff. He made the most of his ability and found it difficult to understand why lesser bowlers than he could not put the ball on a length. A batsman's style tends to reflect his personality and the manner in which Bailey got stuck in with bat and ball illuminated his competitiveness. He would not hold back from bowling a bouncer at a tailender and, when he was angry, made use of an impressive vocabulary of swear words that you would not have expected from someone of his background and with his sense of dignity off the field, for he was a genuinely nice person. He used to get particularly cross when he hit his fingers against the stumps in his delivery. I enjoyed travelling with him because, in addition to learning about the game, I liked the way he planned the journey around visits to pubs *en route*. He also had a childish sense of humour that was never more apparent than the time he threw Fred Trueman into a swimming pool. Trueman never discovered the identity of the culprit, although he threw virtually everybody else in while trying to do so.

The main reason for sharing long car journeys was a perennial lack of money. The limited number of contracted players at the club was augmented by the odd schoolmaster during in the summer holidays, and expenses were saved wherever possible, a policy that extended, on occasion, to us being billeted with opposition committeemen. In the winter, I was fortunate to be employed by an oil company as a travelling salesman. Dick Burge, a prominent businessman who offered me the job, became a friend and in due course sat on my benefit committee. 'Cold calling' does not come easily to a naturally reserved person such as myself and a few of the farmers whom I visited dismissed me curtly and, in some cases, aggressively. The majority were splendidly hospitable, though. They all needed oil of one kind or another and I was able to sign up some new customers. I was able to fit the work around touring, which obviously came first, and gradually built up a group of customers who were interested in sport and came to appreciate the life of a cricketer. From the company's viewpoint, having a recognisable face was a plus point, although

I did not, as was claimed, turn up in farmyards wearing my MCC touring blazer. It was too cold for that and, besides, that kind of paraphernalia did not readily impress farmers who did not follow the game.

Essex were far from a strong team. My development was checked in the sense that I felt, above all, I had to stay in; I could not afford to lose my wicket with a rash shot. At the age of 20 I was one of the best batsmen in the team, in part because Bailey was past his best and close to retirement, but mainly owing to the fact that we had insufficient players of any class. I was selected to tour Pakistan with an MCC Under-25 team under the captaincy of Mike Brearley in 1967 and, through scoring more than 1600 runs that summer, must have been close to being chosen for England. I thought I had a decent chance of being picked for the tour of the West Indies that winter but the selectors, apparently, felt I was not quite ready.

Looking back now, I regret that I did curb my attacking strokes, in particular hitting the ball on the up. I was a better batsman when I went for my shots. Rather than try to be relaxed and score runs, I became determined to score runs as much for the good of the team as myself, which had the effect of making me too concerned about losing my wicket. I allowed seam bowlers to dictate to me more than they should have done, although that also had something to do with batting on indifferent pitches on which the ball nipped about.

If helmets had been standard kit when I was growing up, perhaps I would have played the hook shot and pulled the quicker bowlers more than I did. I did deploy the hook early in my career and learned how to play it effectively. The best exponents of it, including Tom Graveney and Gordon Greenidge, initially went forward but were then able to rock back and control the shot, rolling the wrists and keeping the ball down. However, I admit that I was put off by seeing a number of players – Graham Saville, Phil Whitticase and Mike Gatting come to mind – hit nastily in the face. It was safer to duck – and I wanted to carry on playing. There was also the possibility of being caught off the top edge, so I only tried it occasionally.

The drawback now that everyone wears helmets is that, although these shots can be played without fear of injury, and there is no risk of parents suing over injuries to their children, batsmen are hit far more often as a result of taking their eye off the ball. It is not a case of short-pitched bowling being more prevalent.

The bowlers I found hardest to play at this early stage of my career were primarily the ones who would have troubled any batsman – Fred Trueman and Jack Flavell, the Worcestershire opening bowler who was similar to, if a shade quicker than, Matthew Hoggard. Flavell should have played more Test cricket than he did. Chandrasekhar and Lillee were yet to come. The quintessential English all-rounder who wobbled the ball around at slow-medium, Mike Buss of Sussex or Barry Wood of Lancashire, caused me concern only in the limited-overs game – not because I was especially worried they would take my wicket but because Essex could not permit one or other to bowl their eight or 10 overs for only 25 or 30 runs.

My own batting average and personal statistics never meant a great deal to me, which was to the benefit of the team. The attacking shots I developed, which proved to be my strongest shots throughout my career, were the cut and the drive, particularly off the back foot, with the exception of playing through mid-on. I was too short for that stroke and, besides, other than Ted Dexter and Peter May, few could execute it well. I developed into a strong leg-side player and found I could work the ball through such gaps as there were. Picking the length was never a problem and nor, until I was over 40, were my eyesight or reactions, and then primarily when batting in poor light. So I could play spinners off the back foot without fear of being lbw.

By the time batsmen of the calibre of Graham Gooch and Ken McEwan were playing for Essex, there was less expectation that I should score runs. Yet my mindset was such that, except when I was playing in the one-day game and had to go for my shots – which I relished – I was unable to revert to the attacking cricket of my youth. The two most common modes of dismissal I suffered were lbw and caught; if I was bowled, I reckoned I had succumbed to a fine delivery, more likely than not one that pitched middle stump and hit off. If I was lbw, at least I could accept that my feet were in the correct position. The most aggravating way of being dismissed was to be run out, which, as with a stumping, occurred to me about once a year. I soon learned who was or was not a good judge of a run and ensured that I did the calling on the striker's behalf, especially when Stuart Turner or Nobby Phillip was at the other end. As a junior player, I found that so long as I refused a run with a quick call, that was acceptable to my partner. Alan Lilley once ran me out in a one-day match for Essex, which resulted in a rollicking for him when he himself was out. As for batting with Geoffrey Boycott, I always bore in mind that he was concerned only with reaching the other end of the pitch. So, effectively, I did his calling as well.

Had I played with better batsmen for the first eight or nine years of my career, I believe my game would have been enhanced. I would certainly have been a more consistently attacking batsman and, in all probability, a better one. However, I never entertained any thoughts of moving counties in the way that modern-day cricketers might do. Kevin Pietersen, for instance, moved to Hampshire, citing the fact that he had had to carry Nottinghamshire's batting as the reason. In any case, movement between clubs was more restricted then. Perhaps I was not, as Trevor Bailey surmised, sufficiently self-centred a batsman, but I experienced the unquantifiable satisfaction of leading a county to hitherto unimaginable success.

The rise of Essex in the 1970s and on into the 1980s was due to a number of complementary factors. We had long been a nomadic county, playing on nine out-grounds ranging from Leyton in east London to Westcliff-on-Sea and Southend on the coast. This suited a far-flung membership but it meant the club had insufficient control over the state of the pitches, and considerable expense was incurred in ferrying a caravan of equipment around different venues. The development of the club was enhanced when Chelmsford became a proper headquarters with an administrative base and new pavilion. In 1978, Essex took on Peter Edwards as secretary-manager. He was hard-working, diligent and appreciated the worth of sponsorship and revenue from areas of the game other than the gate. Under him, he had David Collier, who was embarking on a career that would lead to him becoming the chief executive of the ECB.

Above all, decent young players emerged and our overseas signings, Bruce Francis, Keith Boyce, McEwan and Phillip, were not only fine cricketers but good team men. There was not one disagreeable person connected with the club and that was a significant factor in forging a successful first team. Ray

East and Keith Pont provided humour, David Acfield grav-
itas and sufficient objectivity to put up with being made twelfth
man if grass had been left on the pitch and hence would nullify
his off-spin. Stuart Turner, who had been sacked by Bailey,
returned (after Bailey had left) and revelled in the amount of
one-day cricket we were playing. John Lever, who became
another of my best friends in the game, possessed a rare talent
in that he had the ability to swing the ball both ways. He kept
remarkably fit and always wanted to bowl.

If any one person was responsible for shaping the way Essex
came to be regarded around the country, it was Ray East. We
took our cricket seriously and became a highly successful club,
but one with a reputation for humour. East was a natural
comedian with a sense of timing that would not have been
out of place on the stage and the crowds loved him. Even the
umpires found him funny. He was more in demand to speak
at dinners than any of our other players. He came from a
similar cricketing background to me, having had a grounding
in the village game, and stayed with me when he split from
his first wife. I remember that all he brought with him was a
change of clothes and a toothbrush in a plastic supermarket
bag. His simple tastes extended to what he ate. He, Turner
and Brian Hardie were known as the 'scum eaters' because
they would go out together in the evenings and survive on
burgers and a couple of pints when we played an away fixture.
Acfield, Clem Driver and I preferred to go to a decent restau-
rant and would have to put up with them banging on the
window and dribbling tomato ketchup down it as they made
their way back to the hotel with their fast food. More jibes
about our preferences would follow in the dressing room the
next morning when they would ask Acfield how much he had
had to fork out. We took it in good spirit.

Like many a comedian, East was a depressive. His low moments extended to not always wanting to bowl and he retired four years earlier than he should have done because he had had enough, which disappointed me. If his career had not coincided with Derek Underwood's, he would probably have played for England. He could bowl out the opposition on a turning pitch and take, say, two wickets for 70 on a flat one. He was as good a left-arm spinner as Norman Gifford, who played Test cricket at the time mainly because Ray Illingworth, the then captain, had a high regard for him. I had no concerns about fielding at silly point when East was bowling to top-class batsmen and I think he felt that my doing so, after playing in a Test with Underwood, implied that I rated his bowling. It was important that he had a sense of self-belief.

East will always be remembered well beyond Essex. The only time I saw Ken Shuttleworth smile was during a match against Lancashire when East said to him – an England fast bowler, mind – that if he pitched the ball up, he could have his wicket. Shuttleworth fell for this, bowling three half-volleys that East promptly smacked to the cover boundary. Both of them knew what was coming next – the inevitable bouncer from an infuriated bowler. Rather than duck away from the line of the ball, East chose to dive headlong down the pitch, covering himself in dust and dirt as he did so.

He would fool the crowd by pretending to take catches, throwing up a bump ball. He pretended to be shot in his run-up when a car backfired, and on one celebrated occasion, returned to the wicket after tea at Tunbridge Wells, even though he had been given out caught at mid-wicket in spite of his thinking that it was a bump ball. His face hidden behind a helmet, and the Kent players having been made aware of what was going on, he enquired of umpire Jack van Geloven,

'You did say that wasn't out, didn't you, Jack?' The crowd loved this. Keith Pont revelled in all this, too, and Graham Gooch, strange as it may sound to people who saw a dour figure in later years, added his talents as an excellent mimic to the mix. His impersonation of Bob Willis's run-up was wonderfully accurate. Everybody in the team got on with each other. When away from home, we had an unwritten rule that we would meet at the bar at 7 p.m. before splitting up to eat in different places, according to who liked what food. Everyone turned up on time because they knew that, as the captain, I would be buying the first round.

Gooch was the ultimate team man as well as the finest cricketer in the county's history. His fondness for Essex was apparent from an early age and it was immediately clear he was going to be an exceptionally good batsman, one who liked the ball coming on to him above his pads. I was fortunate that he played a great deal of his cricket under my captaincy. When Essex won the Benson & Hedges Cup in 1979, the single most enjoyable day's cricket of my career, Gooch scored a century. We won the County Championship as well, which presaged further success. Contrary to the impression some people may have gleaned, he did not become bored with the county game when he was banned from playing for England; nor, for that matter, did I. That outlook contrasts with the views of some of the best players of more recent times, such as Nasser Hussain.

I have never come across anyone less likely to suffer from nerves before going out to bat than Gooch. Even now, I still get nervous when I play in a benefit game. When Gooch was out, he came back to the pavilion, placed his bat and gloves in his bag and never ever said a word, never swore, whereas Mark Waugh and Allan Border would swear endlessly for a few minutes to get their dismissals out of their systems. He always had time in which to play, which is the sign of a high-class batsman, and it reached the point that slow bowlers – he never referred to them as spinners – were frightened to come on when he was in. He worked hard to correct a failing of moving too far over to the off side against medium pacers, such as Terry Alderman and Mike Selvey, whom he was less happy playing and against whom he suffered some harsh lbw decisions. At a young age he was also a useful wicket-keeper, and should have been deployed by England as an accurate swing bowler in the one-day game. Gooch was 21 when he made his Test debut on a dodgy pitch at Edgbaston against the 1975 Australians, young but mature enough to play. The selectors at the time were seeking young players to take on Dennis Lillee and Jeff Thomson. Is there ever a time when you can say a cricketer is too young? Possibly Brian Close was when he was first chosen for England at the age of 18, but Denis Compton was ready to face all opposition as a teenager.

Overall, I have the highest regard for Gooch in all respects. He is a thoroughly straight person. Like Botham, he is very loyal to his friends but sometimes those loyalties affect his judgements. His belief in Wayne Larkins, a gifted but under-achieving batsman led astray by Colin Milburn, and whom England took to the Caribbean in 1990 under Gooch's captaincy, was a case in point. Gooch comes across as miserable but he's not – he's good fun and has been generous to his friends and his parents, Alf and Rose, who were decent people. He has to be in his own environment with people he knows in order to relax. If he doesn't know everybody, he's wary. Although he likes wine, there was never any danger of him getting drunk because he would fall asleep after a couple of glasses, even round a dinner table.

There are no grey areas in his approach to the game. He believes – too much so, in my view – in work, training and still more training, and does not understand or sympathise with a different attitude. It could be argued, for instance, that if a player's method of playing, training and relaxing is good enough for him to get into the England team, he should not change it. Marcus Trescothick, rocking backwards and forwards at the crease, is a case in point.

I never talked to Gooch about revising his standpoint other than at the selection meeting for the tour of India in 1992–93. I disagreed with him only over that and on his changeable opinions on other players, which meant that he, like Botham, could be too inconsistent to be a selector. Doug Insole, who had a great affection for him, and I could talk to him quietly on such issues. He was a player, and a person, with a lot of self-belief except when he was out of form. Then, as happened at the start of the 1987 season and, prior to that, on the tour of India in 1981–82, when he was given out eight times in eight innings through dodgy umpiring decisions and wanted to go home, he had to be talked into believing he was still a fine batsman. It is easy to say in hindsight that it was a mistake to take him on his last tour to Australia in 1994–95, but who was there who was any better? I'd have backed him to score more runs than anybody in that team. As it happened he didn't, but that kind of loss of form can happen to anybody.

By the time I stood down from the captaincy in 1985, Essex had won the championship twice more, the NatWest Trophy once and the Sunday League three times. I resumed it in 1987 since, although we were champions once more in 1986, Gooch lost form to the point that he thought he was not doing proper justice either to his batting or the leadership of the team. By then, though, I was 43 and I left myself out at times.

Prior to 1987, Essex did not possess a coach other than Ray East, who captained and ran the second XI. When I finally retired, I was asked to coach both the second XI and the first XI. Although my involvement with the first-team players was at weekends only, I was able to have some bearing on the development of Hussain. This was, in a sense, what I had been doing with the younger Essex cricketers for some while now, so it was a natural progression. Moreover, we were successful, becoming champions again in 1991 and 1992, which were my last two seasons with the county, or so I thought at the time.

When I was first invited to coach England in 1992, I demurred. Apart from being offered a three-year contract when I knew at least five years would be needed to make an impression, I would be leaving a club I relished working for and administrators whom I trusted. Not long after, I did, of course, decide to take up that challenge and when I was sacked by England and invited to return to Essex as a 'cricket consultant' – in effect running the club's coaching if not directly overseeing the first team (Alan Butcher was already serving as coach) – I had no idea of the difficulties that would ensue when the standard of the players declined.

The salary I was paid by the Test and County Cricket Board was not enough for me to salt some money away for my retirement. If, for example, I had been managing one of the Premiership football clubs for three years, I would have been able to play golf and do some analysing for television afterwards. I was employed during a fallow period for English cricket, before the advent of central contracts ensured that those at the top, including the coach, would be handsomely rewarded. I could not afford to take two years off and wait for a job to turn up. I had to work.

Interest was shown by other counties but I had no specific offers other than to return to Essex. When I did so in 1995, I discovered the extent to which the club had changed. Several of the best players had either retired or were coming to the end of their careers and some of them, in particular Graham Gooch and Neil Foster, and, from my time as a player, John Lever, were simply irreplaceable. The crowds, which had something of a football mentality about them, were starting to melt away. The County Ground at Chelmsford was beginning to look shabby and in need of some paint, an impression that was enhanced when it was half full. Then Peter Edwards, the secretary/general manager throughout our successful years, died prematurely in 2000. He was an exceptionally efficient and loyal man and I believe that my demotion in the hierarchy – I was by then first-team coach – would not have occurred had he still been alive. The club has not been the same since his death.

Two notable players remained when I returned to Essex – Nasser Hussain and Stuart Law – and Ronnie Irani, who should have had a longer international career, was also there. I had known Hussain since he was 12 when I watched him bowling leg-spinners in the indoor school at Ilford. He was able to bowl to county cricketers and yet lost this ability as he grew. He never comes on to bowl even in benefit or charity matches now. By the time he was good enough to play for Essex in 1987, I was coming to the end of my career and had to decide whether or not I should make way for him. His talent had started to manifest itself when he was at Durham University and there was no point in someone of his ability playing in the second team, so I willingly dropped out of the side. I am grateful that he has not forgotten this. Who knows, that might just have influenced his thinking when he retired from Test cricket in the knowledge that Andrew Strauss did not deserve to lose his place.

When I captained the second XI upon retiring in 1988, he was often in my side, not because he was not making runs in the championship but because he was volatile and found himself demoted. He was always upsetting someone and we thought the best way of disciplining him was to leave him out of the team rather than fine him £300. Some people at the club, including some on the cricket committee, wanted to be rid of him – he was perceived as being too much of a bad influence. He did not hit it off with Neil Foster or Derek Pringle, but he had belief in himself and a thorough determination to do well, and he always wanted to captain Essex and, if truth be known, England. I didn't take any notice of the sharp comments he made to me but some people hold grudges forever. I actually liked him and realised that if we took away his aggression, we would take away the cricketer. Everyone is upset when they are given out and no one was more fed up than I was when I was given out unfairly, but Hussain would take it to extremes. His Gray Nicholls bats would regularly be smashed in the manner of a temperamental pop star chucking his guitar around on stage. Like Mark Ramprakash, he would be very disappointed when he was out and, if someone had a go at him for bashing up the dressing room, he would fire a retort back. I spent a great deal of time standing up for him.

I tried to improve his technique as well. There were certain areas I could work on, not least the need to score more of his runs straighter rather than square of the wicket. He became a lot better at hitting through mid-on and driving straight past the bowler. We emphasised that he must drive towards extra cover and mid-off as much as he could, and managed to prevent his left foot pointing towards cover and his knee bending, a technical failing that accentuated his square driving. He would always listen to advice – he lapped it up – from Gooch, Mark Waugh and me when we spoke about certain types of bowlers and the safest areas in which to score. Like his contemporary, Michael Atherton, he scored a great many of his runs in similar areas – square on the off side and square on the on side. Both players possessed the great asset of watching the ball on to the face of bat, which was not the case with the majority of batsmen. Too many look down the pitch and not at the ball.

Ray Illingworth, when chairman of England selectors, thought Hussain would not succeed in Australia because of his low grip and tendency to score his runs square of the wicket. In retrospect, it was a mistake not to have taken him there when I was coach. As far as the West Indies were concerned, we thought Ramprakash would be more likely to excel in the Caribbean and I, for one, could not believe that he did not do so.

Technically, Hussain, like Atherton, had lots of faults. I knew that Hussain played with his hands too low on the bat handle, but thought it would have been too big an alteration to try to change his grip. He ran the ball to third man far too much, which was a habit formed through playing too much one-day cricket, and one he did not lose for a long while, but he worked out his own strengths, relished the big occasion and, as he claims to have done, made the most of his talent. Any technical failings these two possessed were counter-balanced by their tremendous determination. If I had disciplined Hussain and curbed his technique, I'd have lost a cricketer. The only way he was going to succeed was through development of the attributes he already possessed.

159

When Hussain was made England captain, my one concern was whether he could carry the side with him. If he did, Tim Lamb would not be able to sack him (as he would like to have done). I knew he had the knowledge to succeed. He was the right person at the right time, an individual who showed that, if you're loyal to him, he'll support you. Central contracts suited him – modern players feel they get burned out, whereas, as I have mentioned, older generation batsmen, such as Gooch and me, always wanted to play. However, Hussain having a central contract meant that Essex were an estimated 1500 runs the poorer for his absence. Only Stuart Law would score as many as that in one season. When Hussain came back from a Test match, he could not bat with the intensity of Gooch – he was spent after pouring so much energy into his inter-national performance. Hence he was much better suited to leading England than Essex. The captain of a county has plenty of other involvement and is forever disagreeing with chief executives and attending cricket committee meetings. That amounts to a great deal of hassle, none of which Hussain wanted.

He didn't particularly enjoy fielding or catching practice or getting fit, either. I imagine Duncan Fletcher, when he became England coach, would have told him decisively that he had to show more enthusiasm for his training and fielding. He must have shown a lot more keenness when with England than he did with Essex, otherwise he would not have been made captain. He was cute. He knuckled down.

Once Hussain had made a success of captaining England and then announced his retirement from Test cricket in 2004, I knew he would not want to return to playing county cricket. I would have liked him to stay on for the rest of the season but I think he made the right decision to quit after scoring a century at Lord's. His connection with Essex seems to have come to an end now, although he continues to live in the county and if I asked him to come and cast his eye over a young lad, he would probably do so.

Like Hussain, with whom he did not get on, Law was a prickly person. I first saw him representing Queensland when I was England coach and recommended that he be signed by Essex as our main overseas player. He should have played for Australia regularly for he was a sufficiently classy batsman to have averaged 45 in Test cricket and he was a fine catcher, too. The reason he did not play more than one Test was partly owing to his lifestyle – if I drank as much as him, I'd be dead – and partly because he was, and is, a loner. He was not popular with his fellow Aussies, and particularly not with Shane Warne, who could not stand him. When he played for Essex, he felt that three or four players in the side were not good enough and he was carrying them, and eventually he said so in public. If he had played in my sides of the late seventies and eighties, he would have been more respectful because he would have been surrounded by better players who got on with one another.

When I returned to Essex, I could not understand why there had been so much negative feedback about Irani from Atherton and David Lloyd and, when Irani represented England A, from Mike Gatting. They did not care for him talking to the opposition rather than to his own team-mates. This went a long way towards ending his England career and yet he was a totally committed, noisy and popular cricketer with a rare enthusiasm. In my view, he should have been treated differently from others and was mishandled. These things do not become apparent until players come back from touring. Irani idolises Eric Cantona and calls his dog after him, which indicates where his tastes lie. He is always wheeling and dealing and will end up a millionaire – but he could go broke first.

Irani was not good enough fundamentally to alter the strength of the team on his own, and Hussain's energies were expended elsewhere, particularly after central contracts came into being. In the winter of 2000, the cricket committee, chaired by Graham Saville, one of my oldest friends in the game, agreed with me that Law could not carry the side and that Essex did not have a strong enough pool of players to remain in division one of the championship – only we did not possess the financial resources to do anything about it. I do not believe the advent of two divisions has been to the benefit of the game. The competition has been devalued because a county cannot be said to have won the championship. The club becomes first-division champions, which is not the same thing at all. When Yorkshire won in 2001, I wound them up by saying that just eight other sides could have become champions. There has not been a proper County Championship since it was turned into two divisions. The bigger clubs, in other words those with Test match grounds, prosper through sheer financial strength, as is the case in football. Other clubs are spending too much money trying to stay in division one. The only beneficiaries of this are overseas players and their agents. It has put cricket back and, alas, more of the income that will accrue from Sky's television rights will, inevitably, go towards acquiring personnel who are not England-qualified. Clubs will break a gentleman's agreement not to sign such players, and overseas coaches are interested in short-term signings only. If I were a Northamptonshire supporter, I would much rather see home-grown players nurtured than watch a bunch of mercenaries.

The worry is that some counties will cut back on their

younger age groups rather than give up signing quick-fix overseas players to maintain their status in division one, or in an attempt to gain promotion. Constant emphasis has to be placed on the development of young cricketers but the counties cannot be expected to be self-financing without annual support from the ECB.

I have no objection to first and second divisions in one-day cricket, because it is the longer form of the game in which players are developed that is relevant. I think a better form of mid-season motivation for counties unlikely to win a trophy would be to allocate prize money in all competitions to every club except the one finishing bottom.

By 2000, the cricket committee had deemed I should be called the coach rather than the cricket consultant. The drawback with this, as Doug Insole observed, was that I would take greater responsibility if things went wrong – and they did. We were relegated the following season, finishing bottom after winning our opening match at Leicester by an innings and 9 runs. When Essex struggled, the supporters had no concept of what it was like to watch an ordinary cricket team. Some stayed away and others reacted vociferously.

On my return to the club, I had realised that the captaincy was a problem. Paul Prichard, who had been appointed captain ahead of Nasser Hussain after a split vote, was a likeable person but it is difficult for any discipline to be enforced when the skipper is at the bar all night and is the last one to bed. Alas for Prichard, most of the senior players, including Hussain, told the chairman of the cricket committee that he should be replaced. Saville and I fought this off for quite a while and tried to make Prichard change his ways, but he didn't. In the end, by the time he lost the captaincy in 1998, only Law, Ronnie Irani and I were supportive of him.

Later, there was disquiet from the members over the omission from the side of Peter Such, who at the age of 38 was still the best off-spinner in the country. The problem was that he was a one-dimensional cricketer. He couldn't bat or field well and there was not sufficient turn in the pitches to justify his inclusion.

The out-grounds in Essex, and elsewhere, which were sometimes no more than public parks, were no longer prepared and tended by local groundsmen and became bland and conducive to large scores. Every square in England at the moment is scarified, which means the surface of the soil is loosened – the amount of work that goes on at the end of the year is considerable compared to what occurred in the past – and, of course, there are no uncovered pitches. Hence batsmen are learning to play on pitches on which the ball does not move around or turn. If and when it does, they do not have the technique to cope and they are not prepared to work for runs. Late swing results in a nick to the wicket-keeper. So when seemingly seasoned cricketers tour India and Sri Lanka, they have to be taught how to play spin and not try to score through the off side against Muttiah Muralitharan. It is up to the authorities to allow more variation in pitches and to take into account that all counties can afford proper equipment and covering. To give two examples from my playing days, Gordon Barker, the Essex opening batsman, and Brian Close, the former Yorkshire and England all-rounder, both of whom would be averaging more than 40 in the modern game, finished with career averages that were considerably less than that. In many ways, this indicates how good a batsman Geoff Boycott was, for he had to bat on some dirt tracks in Yorkshire.

In the 1960s, Test grounds were the only venues where

good batting pitches were to be found. Derbyshire produced green surfaces, not least to suit their attack. In Glamorgan, the ball turned. Groundsmen used to take into account the best ways of getting people out and, unless we start to produce pitches that take spin, we are not going to come up with any spinners. Given the way the game is going, it is apparent that five years hence, unless you can bat, you won't be in a first-class side. This applies to wicket-keepers as much as bowlers. If Keith Andrew, Jimmy Binks and Bob Taylor, all highly skilled but ordinary batsmen, were beginning their careers now, they would not be given a game. It is easier to teach someone to keep wicket than it is to bat. Not many people are aware that Alec Stewart, whom I would have loved to have had as wicket-keeper throughout my time as England coach, dropped fewer chances than Jack Russell did when playing for England.

To followers of Essex cricket, though, such insights were seemingly superfluous. They wanted Such to play, regardless of what the pitches were doing, and above all they could not countenance failure or relegation. When problems started to accumulate in 2001, the more vociferous supporters started to behave like football yobs, calling for heads. Appalling comments were posted on the members' web-site. Those people should have realised that our cyclical era of success had lasted for longer than that of some other counties. A handful of members, egged on by the Boundary Club, a group of 200 supporters who raise around £25,000 for the club annually and hence have a voice in the running of it, demanded an extraordinary general meeting. They wanted Law to replace Irani as captain, felt a number of players, Darren Robinson in particular, had under-achieved and that the results were not what they should have been. There was also a feeling, I think, that I was being looked after by old colleagues, such as Insole, Acfield and Saville, in spite of having left the club to coach England; I was a beneficiary of the 'jobs for the boys' syndrome. In my fifth decade at the club, my status was questioned for the first time. I was still the first-team coach and some of those who did the questioning were too young to have seen me play for Essex. I was regarded not as someone who had built up the club but as presiding over its decline. One member of the cricket committee wanted me sacked.

We were beaten by an innings by Kent at Southend in July, which left us very much at the bottom of the first-division table. Prichard did not want to continue as a player, citing a loss of interest in the game. David East, our new chief executive, agreed to meet seven members since they claimed to be representative of the membership as a whole. In retrospect, this was a mistake. Such matters should be resolved in the winter months, not in the middle of the season. Acfield tried to stave off the meeting by resigning as chairman. He had a full-time job to do, did not relish any conflict and reckoned that if he stood down, the problem would diminish. Insole, our president and a man who had done so much for the game over four decades, was taken aback by this disruption and the committee panicked. They felt a sacrifice had to be made to appease these malcontents and decided I should be that person. Gooch would be brought in as coach and, if he decided not to take on the position, someone else would be appointed from outside the county. That, the club knew, would satisfy anyone who supported them.

Saville was given the unpleasant – and, for him, embarrassing – task of telling me that I could work in the Academy, assessing the development of young players, and undertaking scouting assignments. There was already a second XI coach,

John Childs. This was a totally different role from what I had been accustomed to doing. During the summer I would still be working seven days a week but that would come down to sixteen or seventeen hours in January and February. My salary would be cut by half. Since then, it has been cut by half again.

In the modern way, no loyalty was shown to me in spite of my long association with the county. Furthermore, some members and committeemen, people whom I had sat alongside in meetings for two decades, could not comprehend why I was still on the payroll. A number of the twenty to twenty-five general committee members, both at Essex and other counties, hold office merely for the privileges attached, such as car-parking rights, seats in the best surroundings and free drinks, and are fearful of losing these to the extent that they will look after only their own interests. Others, I should add, work selflessly for the good of their clubs.

I still run into some of these people who engineered my removal as coach and I am still polite towards them. They played on my affection for the county, knowing I would not create a fuss. I still feel my work for the county is important – the development of young players is the only way in which Essex will be a force in the game once more. Part of my job specification is to watch club cricket and to look at cricketers who have been recommended to us, such as Alastair Cook, a part of whose development has been down to Derek Randall, my old England colleague who now coaches at Bedford School. Alastair picks things up quickly and is very sensible and level-headed. It is not enough merely to be talented. A cricketer's success is determined by 75 per cent talent, 15 per cent common sense and 10 per cent luck plus a willingness to take advice and look after your own lifestyle. I always gave myself the best possible chance of succeeding as a player in terms of preparation, whereas a batsman who goes in to bat with a hangover is not giving himself a chance. Certainly, a number of cricketers who drank too much in the past would have been better players if they hadn't done so – even the exceptional ones.

In the winter months, squad sessions, which I help run, offer the chance to examine in detail the techniques of the most promising recruits to the Academy at Chelmsford. I do not think we have made one wrong decision over whether or not a young cricketer would make the grade, although the club erred, during the early 1990s, in playing Jon Lewis ahead of Nick Knight. He would have carried our batting for fifteen years, but instead, even after I had had endless telephone conversations with him, we lost him to Warwickshire. Both he and John Stephenson, who wanted to captain a county, left the club while I was with England and I am certain that would not have happened had I still been their coach.

Although in recent years Gooch has worked incredibly hard, raising money himself for the development of young players through organising and speaking at dinners, Essex's financial position is no better than when I was coach. Players brought in from other counties, such as Aftab Habib and Jon Dakin, have not been worth their substantial salaries. The salary structure in the game is of no help. Law, fine player though he was, eventually wanted a package of around £170,000 per annum including air tickets for him and his girl-friend, accommodation and a car, which he was prepared to reduce provided he was given the captaincy. Not many counties could have met those demands and, not surprisingly, following an outburst on local radio about the lack of quality on the playing staff, he ended up playing for one that had the financial clout of possessing a Test match ground, Lancashire. Essex simply cannot afford crackerjack overseas players.

The fact that Gooch has opted to revert to his media work and coach only the batsmen is a further indication that the club is not in a position to regain its eminence of old. This could conceivably bring about a seismic change in coaching structures in England. Gooch, who enjoyed his summarising for 'Test Match Special' in the past, will also be concentrating on corporate hospitality commitments and promotional work for the club, which he will do well. He has found, as I did, that a cricket coach's role is very different from that of a football coach. For much of the day you would be better off assisting the development of young players rather than tearing your hair out in the changing room. The frustrating element of the job lies in not being able to influence events on the field in the way that a football manager can do through tactics over a much shorter period. I once spoke about this to Sir Bobby Robson, who, when he was manager of Ipswich Town, took part in a benefit match against Essex. He was competitive and enthusiastic and would have been a decent club cricketer, but cricket coaching would have frustrated him.

Counties have mistakenly felt that football-style coaches from overseas can be their saviours. This is all of a piece with the hiring and firing/promotion and relegation mentality that now exists in the game and has afflicted counties, such as Essex, that have had success only in the modern era. The drawback of employing such a coach or manager is that, quite apart from his possessing a short-term outlook and sucking a considerable amount of money out of the game, he will not be in the country when the real coaching is undertaken, from January to April. Such individuals like to exercise total control over the selection of their teams, whereas in Essex our cohesion and triumphs have been based on the captain having the power of selection, assisted by specialist coaches in batting, bowling, wicket-keeping and fielding. I continue to believe firmly in this process. There would be more stability in county cricket if all captains had that power and retained their positions for longer than a handful of years.

What is the future? The club has fared no better since I was moved on. It will belong in the first division only if gifted young cricketers, who have a feel for the club and the game, can be nurtured. As for me, when I look back over more than forty years in the game, I ponder on the old adage that a person should not go back to a place where he knew success and fulfilment. I did, and discovered a changed environment. The Essex of the 1970s and 1980s could not be replicated. Then again, I had to work and I do still thoroughly enjoy coaching, especially the youngsters who attend the Essex Academy, and watching cricket, and reckon that I shall always be involved in the game in some capacity.

I remain a countryman. I could never live in a town, still less a city. My home near Dunmow, where I have lived since 1984, is a former rectory that became a private dwelling in 1870 because it was considered by the Church to be too small for the incumbent rector. I have an acre of garden in which I grow all manner of produce for the house. I still follow the pursuits of my youth in Cambridgeshire and dislike any governmental interference in rural ways. I beat and occasionally shoot on the farms and in the woods around my home, which I enjoy even more than being on the golf course. I relish the rhythms of farming life. As I walk around the village, I know it is still a community, albeit one threatened by the planned expansion of Stansted Airport. For the moment, Sue and I would not wish to live anywhere else, although we have too much space now that both our daughters are grown up and living in London, and are aware that we shall have to move to somewhere smaller in our retirement and old age. In the coming years, I would like to see something of Europe, Scotland and Ireland, and would rather do so in the summer than in the winter months. I do not think I shall quite manage to reach a half century in terms of years with Essex, but my enthusiasm for the game, even come the end of September each year when I have had my fill of long car journeys to distant grounds, remains constant. I do not anticipate that I shall ever lose it.

CHAPTER 8

THE FUTURE
OF THE GAME

The falling away of standards in county cricket, which had become apparent to me by the time I became England coach, coincided with the resurgence of football and the inauguration of the Premiership. Even the quality of overseas signings was not what it had been owing to the growth of international fixtures. In particular, young players were not progressing as quickly as once they had, in part because just two consequential pools of talent were available to be tapped by the county clubs. One was the public schools, in which the game had not been curtailed and grounds not sold off for development as, disastrously, had been the case in much of the state sector. Team sports generally breed less selfish individuals, a fact that seems to have been completely overlooked. In the private sector, Felsted, until my old team-mate Gordon Barker retired as its professional, nurtured future England players, such as Derek Pringle and Nick Knight. Tonbridge was synonymous with Kent, Millfield with Somerset and Radley with any number of counties. Numerous other examples abounded. If the Mays,

Cowdreys and Dexters of old were not forthcoming, at least they produced players competent enough to play county and, conceivably, Test cricket.

Outside the public schools, however, it was altogether a different matter. Kwik cricket and other such innovations compensated for the absence of the proper game, but only to a certain extent. Amateur clubs have had to take up the slack, sending the most promising players on to the county academies.

Of the 300 or so teenagers whom I watch each year at Chelmsford, around half are not contemplating taking up the game as a career, and would not be good enough to do so, anyway. As for the rest, a handful may have a chance of progressing in the game. It is generally possible to tell when a boy is 16 or 17 years old whether he is going to have a cricketing future. Observing Pringle, Nasser Hussain, Paul Prichard and Neil Foster at those ages, I could see that they were cricketers in the making. Alastair Cook was another.

What to look for in a young cricketer? Fielding is such an important aspect of the game now that it is important to check how athletic a young person is in practice. Colin Cowdrey and Tom Graveney may have been fine specialist slips in their 'box,' as we say, but these days they would be expected to run and dive around with everybody else. A latter-day Colin Milburn would not be chosen for a one-day match, however much he might devastate an attack, because he would not be considered mobile enough. I seek to ensure that a bowler does not have a mixed action so as to avoid back trouble later in his career. I look for accuracy, rhythm, whether he can swing the ball and a high action. Bowling off the wrong foot is of no concern. The wonderful career that Mike Procter enjoyed bore testimony to that. Ideally, batsmen should demonstrate a sense of timing, flair, balance and the ability to play forward or back.

I reckon to watch a boy of 16 or 17 for ten to fifteen minutes and then make a judgement. I would also reckon to be right most of the time. Apart from when I was coaching England, not one young cricketer has joined Essex since I became captain in 1974 without my opinion having been sought and I am glad to say we have not erred in terms of releasing anybody. The hardest aspect of a county coach's job is to tell an individual he is not going to make the grade, but then it is necessary to do so in order to be fair to the person concerned when he is still young enough to embark on a different career.

I tell young cricketers to listen to their elders – not necessarily betters, but players and umpires who are experienced and who will willingly impart advice after play. One of the saddest aspects of modern-day cricket is that there is little fraternisation with opponents and, especially, with seasoned cricketers. I learned from listening to Brian Close, Fred Trueman, Ken Barrington, Peter Parfitt and John Murray. All were long-serving Test players and gregarious men. Later, I would send a young batsman to an umpire to discuss with him how he was out and what he thought of a particular innings. Umpires, the vast majority of whom were first-class cricketers, have a wonderful knowledge of the game and are rarely in any rush to leave the ground in the evening to return to their lonely overnight accommodation to eat on their own. They tend not to turn down the offer of a beer or two.

Alas, the advent of overseas coaches has ruined socialising between opposing players. In my experience, many lack a sense of humour and frown on mixing and drinking with the opposition. Post-play warm-downs in the swimming pool are in vogue now to the extent that a touring party will choose hotels in England not on the basis of star ratings but whether there is a gym or a pool. Concerns over drink-driving may well have had something to do with less time spent at the bar. An individual such as Ray East, who still took his cricket seriously, would not be tolerated by dour coaches such as Daryl Foster and Kepler Wessels – and probably not by Duncan Fletcher, either. It is a great shame. No one would advocate returning to an age of excessive drinking, other than certain fast bowlers who believed that downing pints was their prerogative and that they could work it off the following morning through a long spell, but the approach now is not balanced, either.

With the notable exception of John Bracewell, who turned Gloucestershire into such a competitive one-day team, foreign coaches tend to stay in county cricket for a short time only and hence are not concerned about long-term development of young players. They are after instant success to justify their inflated salaries. As a result, too many second-rate overseas players, EU and Kolpak signings who have freedom of contract, and who may well have reached maturity, are blocking the emergence of English talent. This is a matter that has to be addressed urgently, although I do not anticipate that David Collier, whom I got to know when he began his career in cricket administration as assistant secretary of Essex, will be able to deal with it in his capacity as chief executive of the ECB. There are too many legal ramifications and too much protection for the players under European law.

I have long insisted to the Essex committee that our overseas signings have to be of the highest standard. Only one, Hugh Page, the South African medium pacer, has turned out not to be a success, and that was on account of injury. The key generally is to go for up-and-coming players, preferably

Australians and South Africans, who have a will to win. We have tended not to employ Asians and West Indians, chiefly because we have been uncertain about how they will turn out in the long term. Andy Roberts, for example, was a brilliant fast bowler for Hampshire for a while but lost interest. Although much the same could have been said of that county's star batsman, Barry Richards, that had a lot to do with his not playing Test cricket and he still batted consistently. There have, of course, been exceptions. Allan Border was captain of Australia when he joined Essex and Salim Malik – 'honest Sal' as we jokingly called him while a bevy of Pakistanis drove around in his sponsored car – was an experienced batsman who proved to be a decent signing.

Two high-class overseas players per club, which was the norm in the 1970s, would improve the standard of county cricket, without question, but that is not practicable in an era when so many Test matches are played. As it is, the domestic game has become an irreconcilable muddle of short-term signings to the extent that identity and unity has been lost and members and followers of the game cannot keep up with which county has taken on which player. Michael Bevan, the Australian batsman, is a case in point. In 2004 he joined Kent, his fourth county, for a few weeks as a locum overseas signing, and yet he was dropped and returned home before his contract expired. All the while, a young home-grown cricketer was kept out of the first team. What a waste of money.

The other concern about such a myopic approach, of course, is the expense. I have no objection to a world-class cricketer, a Ponting or a Warne, earning vast sums from county clubs. They bring spectators through the turnstiles and their knowledge of the game should be of considerable benefit to up-and-coming young players. I do object to second-rate performers being extravagantly paid. Clubs – and Northamptonshire come to mind as one that is not concentrating sufficiently on nurturing England-qualified cricketers – should not take hand-outs from the ECB for granted; nor should minor counties. They should be promoting youngsters for the purpose of becoming county cricketers, not fielding former first-class players unless they are undertaking coaching as well.

Followers of the game have been not so much overlooked in all of this as completely disregarded. I am quite sure that county members prefer their subscriptions, even though they do not amount to as much as they should, to go towards the development of cricketers born or educated locally. After all, an Essex supporter can empathise more readily with some-body raised in Clacton than in Coventry or Canberra. Even if there is little loyalty left in the game, as in the workplace generally, one would hope that some players today still have a feel for the counties of their birth. Graham Gooch's affec-tion for Essex was revealing in his performances when he returned from a Test match, however exhausted he must have been. A player who has come up through the junior levels of his club should surely be appreciative in return and not seek a move merely for financial benefit.

We have to give more attention to what the public wants to watch and to encourage children to attend by letting them into county grounds for free. If a Test match is over in three days, a one-day international should be staged on the Sunday, although when I suggested this to David Graveney in his capacity as chairman of selectors, he retorted that he was having enough rows with Duncan Fletcher and did not want to have another one. Test matches are expensive events to attend and we are, after all, in the entertainment business. Not providing county cricket on Saturdays is a case in point. Four-day championship matches start on Wednesdays and sometimes are finished by Friday evening, if not Thursday. I believe three-day matches, long advocated by Essex as the ideal form of first-class cricket in England, is what traditional followers of the game in England would still like to see. I have lost count of the number of four-day fixtures I have attended in which the progress made by lunchtime on the second day is equivalent to what had occurred in years gone by on the evening of the first day. Four-day cricket is a watered down version of championship cricket and I have to admit to finding it a bit tedious.

I am also concerned about batsmen having a limited number of innings. If I was out for a duck on a Wednesday, I knew I would have two or three more innings that week. Similarly, the bowlers wanted to bowl and take wickets. The Sunday League is derided to some extent now but I enjoyed it because its short format was such that I was forced to hit my way out of a defensive mindset or, perhaps, a lean period. After having to battle for runs on a turning pitch or in difficult conditions, facing bowlers who had no slip fielders in place, could not deliver bouncers and who came in off restricted run-ups was not difficult. I thought that I could not get out unless I hit the ball up in the air.

At least Twenty20 cricket has provided the general public with a competition that they want to watch. I was only surprised it had not been dreamed up earlier. When I was a boy, games of this duration used to be staged on Parker's Piece in Cambridge, and great fun they were, too. It is inevitable that there will be a considerable number of 20 overs a side international matches in future, the downside being that, even in such a cricket-loving city as Calcutta, this could affect attendances for Test matches. Improvisation is needed in the first-class game and this competition provides it. The best players are still the ones who score the most runs and take the most wickets. Mark Ramprakash continues to bat stylishly and Andrew Symonds still strikes the ball conventionally and as hard as anyone – one six he struck during the 2004 season went 50 yards above my head in the crowd. Batsmen have become more adept at chasing totals and the white balls, once they have softened up after the first 15 overs, can be belted farther than conventional ones. The manufacturers have never discovered the reason for this and say the balls are not made in another way, but the difference is pronounced in England, more so than abroad. I have noticed also that the seam is sharper and can cut the fingers when taking a sharp catch. The players, although sceptical initially, thoroughly enjoy this form of the game and for the spectators, there is no messing around with the timing. Close of play is when it is advertised, unlike in all the other competitions down the years. Slow over rates have had a detrimental effect that has been lasting.

More consideration has to be given to the appeal of the game. On too many occasions play has not taken place owing to bad light or a slightly squelchy outfield. If conditions are too wet for the seamers' run-ups, the spinners can still bowl. I am loath to criticise umpires, many of whom are old friends and colleagues, but they do tend to put the interests of the players before those of the general public.

Dickie Bird was a fine Test match umpire, but a forceful captain could sometimes bully him. I could say to him, 'It's bloody dark out here, Dickie,' and out would come his light meter. After an inspection of the square, he would call the two captains over and tell them he thought it was a bit wet. They could respond that the best plan would be not to play until the ground had dried out. Alan Whitehead or John

Hampshire were not so easily influenced. Perhaps Dickie Bird was worried about the marks he would be given by the captains at the end of a match, which were sent to Lord's. He had seen what had happened to David Constant, whom the TCCB had not supported as they should have done following complaints from Pakistan.

In fact, I never wanted him to stand in a county match I was involved in for a different reason. The opposition had to be bowled out twice over three days and he was renowned as a 'not outer' – someone who always gave the batsman the benefit of the doubt over an appeal. For that reason, he became more acceptable as a Test match official than Ray Julian, for instance, who generally favoured the bowlers over lbw decisions. Bird achieved his notoriety through being a nice sort. What he has made out of the game, financially and in terms of his fame, has been disproportionate to his status within it.

The best umpires are the ones who keep control of the game and who command the respect of the players. Still, English officials remain the most highly regarded in the world. The standard overseas was so poor in my playing career that, although I 'walked' when I knew I had hit the ball in a match in England, I would not do so anywhere else. I was the victim of too many awful decisions for that, especially in New Zealand. A batsman knows whether or not he has edged the ball 90 per cent of the time and, in England at any rate, it is in his best interests to walk. Word gets around if he does not and the next time there is a questionable decision, he will not receive any sympathy from the umpire.

Umpiring standards improved in Australia and the West Indies in inverse proportion to the behaviour of players. When I started in the game, a fielder's word over a catch was accepted. If he claimed to have taken a catch, the batsman usually did not question it. Only once did I take issue with an opponent. John Steele, who was then with Leicestershire and who later became an umpire, reckoned he had caught me off his own bowling in a county match. I was not so certain, stood my ground and was given not out. These days, alas, you would not take anybody's word in a Test match over a claimed catch. Players, particularly wicket-keepers, appeal for everything and that constitutes cheating as much as a batsman remaining at the crease after nicking the ball, yet this is considered part of the game. No wonder David Shepherd noticeably failed to call a number of no-balls during one Test – he was having to concentrate so hard on all the appeals by the close fielders at the other end of the pitch. Ethics change when players are paid a lot of money to win a match, which is one of the less appealing legacies of Kerry Packer's World Series Cricket.

Even if some umpires are not particularly competent, one would hope there is no bias in their decision making. Dickie Bird would have it that to refer to 'neutral umpires' is an insulting phrase, given that the whole purpose of their adjudication is to be fair to both teams. Anyway, the introduction of an international panel has been a considerable boon for the game, if not always for individual umpires. It has always been a solitary, lonely life and that has become exacerbated for those who travel abroad to stand in Test matches. On the county circuit, umpires often end up eating on their own because their colleagues are staying in a different area. Consuming sandwiches left over from tea while spending the evening in bed and breakfast accommodation is not for me. What an existence! For that reason I never even contemplated becoming an umpire when my playing days were over.

I am not that upset about the television deal that has resulted in Test cricket being exclusively shown on Sky. Terrestrial companies wanted to cover certain matches only, whereas Sky, whose coverage has been commendable, will be concentrating on other areas of the game, such as championship cricket, Twenty20 games and women's cricket, as well as bringing us overseas tours. If Channel Four had offered the ECB just a few million pounds less than Sky offered, it would have gained the rights. As it was, Channel Four's offer was well short and left the ECB with little choice but to take a chance that Sky will not manage to dictate a lower price when the rights to international cricket come up for renewal four years down the line. The BBC would do well to revert to its sports coverage of old rather than continually spending money on dreadful soap operas. With any luck, the game will attract more money because England are doing well. What I do find concerning, however, is that the counties who are continuing to find money to spend on Kolpak and EU players are likely now to receive even more from the ECB's pot.

Tours will continue to be short and crammed with Test matches because that is what Sky, as well as the players, want. The expense of having television crews and cameramen filling in time in expensive hotels while England play some meaningless up-country fixture does not appeal. Television producers reckon that constant international cricket maintains a momentum, and cricketers want to see more of their families. A six-month tour of the kind I had to endure as a young, newly married man would not be tolerated nowadays. The flip side of this is that players are commencing a Test series unprepared, as occurred in South Africa in 2004–05. Not only is there no time for anyone who has had a break from the game to find any form, but no opportunity for anyone not in the England team to break into it. Gareth Batty and Paul Collingwood did not have a chance to do so on that trip. The ideal length for a tour, I think, is ten weeks with two four-day practice matches at the start, a Test every fortnight, and only one occurrence of back-to-back Tests.

ENGLAND PRESENT

Raymond Illingworth and I should have taken notice of Michael Vaughan's potential and he ought to have played Test cricket earlier than he did. I did watch him bat for Yorkshire when I was coaching England and could see that he moved into good positions at the crease, was balanced, had the ability to improvise, and could cover the ball that nipped back from outside off stump. Those are the attributes required for Test cricket. He was evidently sufficiently competitive, in his quiet way. The main reason, I think, for his not coming to our attention earlier than he did was because he had never been a heavy scorer in county cricket.

In my view the reason for that was because he was playing much of his cricket at Headingley. On up-and-down pitches a batsman will lose confidence. Even so, I am surprised that Illingworth, living as he did near to the ground, and possessing an intimate knowledge of cricket within Yorkshire, did not become aware that here was a batsman in the making. Eventually, Vaughan was chosen for an England tour in 1999, but by then he was 25 and was still not regarded as the kind of cricketer who, in a short period and against the best team in the world, would progress to another level.

The square at Headingley was a constant problem in the 1990s. I recall from when I started out in the game how difficult it was to cope with batting on poor pitches. I played on a variety of out-grounds and when Essex moved on to an even surface at a venue such as The Oval, I struggled to hit the ball off the square. Others would try to slog their way out of trouble. The significant aspect of playing in those poor conditions was that spin bowlers would develop more readily. That is no longer the case. Vaughan the bowler is the product of too much cricket on the bland pitches that have superseded those cut on the festival grounds, which mostly are no longer used for first-class cricket. Groundsmen, in addition to taking pride in their work, now have to compete with each other in a league table of performance. Vaughan is quite capable of bowling tidy off-spin to a containing length and will take the odd important wicket, but England will not be able to compete with India and Pakistan on the sub-continent in the future unless sharper spinners of the ball can be unearthed.

In other respects, Vaughan has undoubtedly benefited from growing up in Yorkshire. The vast majority of cricketers who have learned their cricket there know the game. They have a grounding that is not acquired in the south. In part, this is passed on from their fathers and is also gleaned through common sense. This is akin to the grounding that Australians such as Ricky Ponting receives, given that cricket is their national sport. You can sense that when Vaughan switches his field around, he instinctively knows who should go into which position, although his concentration on his own ground fielding is not always all it might be. An opening batsman can be forgiven for thinking about his own game when the opposition are eight wickets down. I have seen Geoffrey Boycott in a world of his own in that situation, in the full knowledge that shortly he will have to face some high-class fast bowling.

One failing Vaughan has in an otherwise admirably correct technique is, coincidentally or not, similar to the shortcomings inherent in Michael Atherton and Nasser Hussain. He has a tendency to play too square on both sides of the wicket, which probably derives from having been taught to be sideways on in his youth. His front foot points too much in the direction of extra cover, which means that he cannot pivot to knock the ball away to the leg side with as much flexibility as is desirable. I would like to see him drive the ball back to the bowler more than he does. Besides, the straight drive is one of the most pleasing of all shots. There was a saying when I was young that the off side was a girl's side, the leg side a man's side. All the Australian batsmen hit half volleys wide of mid-on or straight back to the bowler. If these pitch six inches outside off stump they should be dispatched through extra cover, which is best achieved with the full face of the bat.

For Vaughan, as for anybody else, the exception to this rule would be when facing Muttiah Muralitharan, whom I would not think of hitting through the covers on account of the spin he imparts. I would stick my front pad outside the line of off stump, which would mean I would not be lbw, and try to strike him to leg. One of the difficulties I had when with England was that there was scant time to assist Atherton and Hussain among others in this detailed way because I was so tied up sorting out peripheral matters. I am not advocating too much tinkering because there is quite enough of that already from any number of coaches, but Duncan Fletcher now has the time and opportunity for specialist, common-sense coaching.

Credit to Fletcher for having realised that Vaughan could succeed, mentally and technically, in Test cricket. He is deserving of more plaudits still for picking out Marcus Trescothick, another batsman who – in spite of playing on perhaps the most true square in the country at Taunton – was far from a heavy scorer in the County Championship. True, he had performed fairly well for England Under-19s, but seemingly had not taken his game forward. I think Fletcher appreciated that he had the desire and temperament to be able to play at the highest level and that he could overcome his tendency to put on weight. His fondness for sausages was such that he did not eat proper hot lunches and dinners until he was 18. Before the Under-19 tour to Sri Lanka, he could not reach the required level twelve in his fitness assessment, only managing to get up to level six. A combination of that and the heat meant he could not stay in the middle after reaching 50.

Trescothick's good fortune was that Duncan Fletcher was still coaching Glamorgan when he made a century against them for Somerset. The main criticism he has faced has been over his relative lack of foot movement. Yet left-handers do not have to move their feet a great deal. In the main, a right-arm bowler will be slanting the ball across them. If it pitches on off stump and bowls the batsman, it will have had to move back a long way. So long as Trescothick, a chunky man, transfers his weight forwards and backwards effectively, he will not have to concern himself too much about the position of his feet. He has an unruffled presence about him at the crease, for sure.

It is also easily overlooked that his struggles against the Australians have come about because he has had to contend with world-class bowlers. I reiterate the point that I made about my own difficulties against Dennis Lillee – opponents of that calibre will always dismiss specialist batsmen. What is important is to ensure that runs are notched up when conditions are favourable for batting. Trescothick's effectiveness lies in his ability to make an unbeaten 60 by lunch on the opening day of a Test, even though the over rate is not conducive to quick scoring. He is recognised as a dangerous opponent. Then, when a spinner comes on in the afternoon, he will sweep him exceptionally well and make any predatory fielder at silly point aware that he will drill the ball in that direction. From my observations, I would regard his technical weakness as more to do with his hands than his feet. He does not allow the ball to come to him because he plays it in front of his eyes, not underneath them.

He holds his catches well at first slip and should continue to work on his fiddly seam bowling, which will be invaluable if it is of sufficient standard to enable England to field just four specialist bowlers, as most teams do nowadays. This is an aspect of the game that is often overlooked. The importance to a team of possessing batsmen who can bowl is relevant in first-class cricket as much as in the one-day game. Trescothick's success emphasises the necessity of watching county cricket, even though Duncan Fletcher appears to disregard it. Ian Bell and Ed Smith, with whom I wasn't impressed, seemingly were afforded the opportunity to play Test cricket in 2004 and 2003 respectively more because of the weight of runs they had scored in county matches rather than any evaluation of their techniques. So was Rob Key, whom I am not convinced has what it takes, either. He possesses the right sort of humour for a dressing room but I don't think he can walk past a pie shop too often, although provided he is quick on his feet, as Colin Cowdrey was for a similarly bulky man, that in itself should not be of concern. He can strike the ball all round the wicket but has a tendency to play around his front pad, his head moving too far towards cover, as the South Africans have discovered. His dismissal in the final Test of the 2004–05 series at Centurion, leg before walking across his stumps, was an exact illustration of this. I often relate batting to boxing in terms of moving into the right positions. When I returned to Essex in 1995, a kick-boxer was employed to get the players fit as part of the winter training programme. This had not happened before and did not go down too well with the pros, but it had its purpose.

Ed Joyce, Jason Gallian and Mark Wagh, whom I thought to be a better prospect than his Warwickshire team-mate Bell, need to be properly assessed in championship cricket, although the preferred means of advancement is the National Academy. It can be inferred from the tremendous progress of Andrew Strauss that this has been proven to be successful, yet this also says something about county cricket, for he was a solid run-maker for Middlesex. Although he can display the same weakness as Trescothick in terms of pushing at the ball in front of his body rather than letting it come to him, he showed in South Africa that he generally plays it under his eyes. I can see no reason why he should not continue to have a profitable Test career apart from the possibility that he might put on weight. He must possess an equable temperament and does not appear to allow success or failure to concern him unduly. He takes a proper step forward or back, maintains a good head position but his tendency to hit the ball in the air between the slips and cover always means that the bowler is given a chance.

I thought Joyce was the better prospect and he might well have been chosen for England ahead of Strauss had he been eligible. Even so, plenty of people are wondering now why Strauss was not selected earlier than he was. I am not at all sure that he should have been. He would not necessarily have had the same success. After his wonderful series in South Africa in 2004–05 – forget the two ducks, think of the three centuries

– bowlers will have noted his tendency to lose his wicket to catches in the ring between the slips and cover. The dismissals will have been beamed around the world and you can be sure that the ball on or just outside off stump tempting him into a front-foot drive is the one that is seen as the telling delivery.

The blossoming opening partnership between Trescothick and Strauss has, of course, meant that Vaughan has gone down the order. As captain, Vaughan has found already that his wicket is the one most prized by the opposition, who feel, rightly or wrongly, that England's innings will be destabilised if he is out cheaply. In South Africa, Graeme Smith, his opposite number, could sense how perturbed he was by fussy umpiring over bad light and the worth of floodlights, and played on it. Vaughan normally has an unruffled presence but he was evidently tired by the end of the tour and his batting was suffering as a consequence. So his concentration in his final innings that effectively brought about a draw at Centurion – and ensured victory in the series – was thoroughly laudable.

I thought before the series started that England would win 3-0. South Africa, in my opinion, are an average team. Smith did not have a particularly effective run with the bat because the English bowlers had worked out that he tends to shovel the ball to leg and swings his arms through the line when given some width outside off stump. The batting depends too much on Jacques Kallis, who is, admittedly, one of the four or five best batsmen in the world. Shaun Pollock is the only member of the attack who could be expected to trouble the foremost players in the opposition and even he is no more or less than the type of bowler you would expect to face at Test level. Makhaya Ntini is a hard-working trier and Andrew Hall a good county bowler rather than a Test cricketer.

England under-performed to a certain extent. Individual

achievements won us an enjoyable series. Another aspect of the matches that I noticed was how few coloured, Indian and black spectators attended the five Tests. The cost of tickets might well have been a factor in this. I would think there needs to be an intensified drive by the United Cricket Board to attract diverse people from a football-loving nation; a bit like the ECB in a some ways. Ntini, you would have thought, might have had a talismanic effect, given his success, but that does not appear to have been the case.

Such individuals are hugely important. There is no question that the cricketer whom England will be primarily dependent on for several years is Andrew Flintoff. It is no exaggeration to say that the interest he creates will be worth millions of pounds to English cricket. He looks like a hero – and strikes the ball like one. The game has been in need of a glamorous figure and, creditably, he had the good sense to realise that if he shed weight and became sufficiently dedicated, he would be well rewarded. In addition to attracting youngsters to the game, he creates interest for corporate entertainment and hence brings more revenue into the game.

There is no use resisting comparisons with Ian Botham, whom I regard, along with Garry Sobers, Imran Khan and Mike Procter as one of the four finest all-rounders to have played the game. Both are, or have been, dangerous bowlers because of their ability to swing the ball, good, athletic catchers and attractive batsmen, full of fun. Botham was my sort of person although I would not go out drinking with him – that would finish me off. Such comparisons are a part of the game played out by spectators and the media. Suffice to say that theirs have been the first names England captains have entered on their teamsheets. If Flintoff's tally of Test wickets falls 100 short of Botham's, he will have had a very fine career.

Possessing a central contract will keep Flintoff going. He should not have to play against Zimbabwe – who should? – or Bangladesh, for he will have to be kept sufficiently fit to be a frontline seamer, bowling 17 overs a day in addition to going in no lower than five or six in the order – Duncan Fletcher sensibly has sent out the unequivocal message that he is a middle-order batsman – and holding the catches of a high-class slip fieldsman. There has never been any danger of him thinking of himself as a tailender. He plays the way he thinks the public wants him to play, taking the attack to the opposition. He will bat on his own terms and will fail at times, but must continue to strike the ball in a manner in which he can turn a game in a short space of time. He should not be planning to construct an innings like those going in ahead of him, or concern himself with his average. He is not going to finish his Test career averaging 45 – 35 to 40 should be expected of him. The decision to send him home for an operation before the one-day internationals started in South Africa was the correct one. The 2005 series against Australia was infinitely more important.

Opponents react to his presence in the same way they did when Graham Gooch came to the wicket. He is similarly feared by bowlers to the extent that they cannot bowl properly at him. At county level, Gooch could be said to have 50 runs to his name before he actually hit a ball. Opposition attacks know that good length balls can disappear to the boundary – often, in Flintoff's case, over it. Strange as it may sound, that is a part of his defence as well.

Any comparison with Botham does not extend to their type of bowling. Flintoff does not swing the ball to the same extent but hits the pitch hard on the back of a length. He is the ideal bowler for the kind of hard surface that is to be found in the

Caribbean or for uneven surfaces such as at Headingley. In due course he will learn reverse swing and to reverse swing his yorker.

Other than that, the only way in which his game can improve is for him to be more selective in his shot-making. He plants his front foot forward too much and needs to be quicker on his feet, as if he were a boxer. Otherwise he will be beaten by a bowler as unerring in accuracy and as capable of bowling a reverse yorker as Glenn McGrath. He will find opponents will try to restrict his scoring and that he will be given the odd feeder ball wide of off stump, and the occasional bouncer, in the hope that he goes after them. The manner in which his game has come on over a period of two or three years, the fact that he no longer bowls too short unless, it would seem, under instruction to do so from his captain, is astonishing. He has been given time to mature in the Test team in a way in which could not have happened if he had still been playing county cricket. He has been provided with the stage he desires and, like Botham, he is very much a team man.

How I wish I had had performers like that to choose from when I was coaching England. The best cricketer from my time, Graham Thorpe, remains technically the finest batsman in the country. But for his marital problems he would probably be averaging 45 in Test cricket now. He is a selfish person, which is sometimes to a batsman's advantage. I could never persuade him to bowl at others in the nets and he did not particularly enjoy county cricket, regarding it as a necessary chore if he was to play for England. In retrospect, what I should have done was to put him in charge of team discipline. If I told him not to wear shorts for breakfast, for instance, he would appear wearing shorts. A coach and a captain have enough to do without having to deal with that. His anti-establishment streak was not nasty, but indicative that no one in authority would get anywhere with him if he did not respect them. He did not make friends easily but he got on with Nasser Hussain and Mark Ramprakash. I gained the impression, though, that he listened to what I was saying and I like to think he was disappointed when I left.

Apart from Thorpe, the one person who has continued to merit a place in the England team since my day is Mark Butcher. He has worked hard at his game, not least with his father, Alan. He needed to improve his technique against spin to pick the length better and to play with softer hands so as to prevent edged shots carrying to slip and the bat and pad being thrust at the ball. To some extent he has extended his international career through the standing he attained with his unbeaten match-winning innings of 173 against Australia in 2001, but he deserves credit for adjusting his game. His catching, however, remains iffy. Nasser Hussain was a far better slip fielder but preferred to organise his players (and, to their irritation in mid-over, his bowlers) from mid-off when England captain. The competition from Joyce, Bell and Kevin Pietersen is such that Butcher will need to be markedly consistent for the remainder of his career.

Pietersen has abundant talent and flair, that much is self-evident. His temperament is also impressive, for not everybody could have coped with the stick he received from South African crowds when he began his international career playing against his homeland. I have been impressed by the way he takes the attack to the opposition. The fact that he has chosen to play for England indicates the mess the game is in in South Africa. It was not clear whether the captain, the selectors, the coach or the United Cricket Board was selecting their team, and the muddle is likely to continue. Clearly it is imperative that more black and coloured cricketers are brought into first-class cricket. There has to be one criterion for selection at Test level – if you are good enough, you play, if you are not, you don't. What would a non-white cricketer feel if he had not been picked for his country on merit? South Africa can ill afford to lose players of the calibre of Pietersen, as cricket followers are only too aware. I suspect this was an additional reason for the hostility shown towards him.

Technically, Pietersen will struggle in Test cricket if his head continues to over-balance too far towards cover. He moves a long way across the stumps. That is acceptable so long as he plays straight, but he could well have difficulties against bowlers who have the ability to pitch the ball on off stump and hit it. On the other hand, he will excel in a country such as India because he strikes spinners so cleanly. The fact that he is one-eyed about his future can only work in his favour, but his keenness to earn more money might not do so. I feel he would have been better off joining a club other than Hampshire. The Rose Bowl pitches are not conducive to building an innings – better to have taken a lesser offer from a county with a square where the pitches are properly bedded down. As for wanting to play under Shane Warne, who evidently rates him and recommended him, that can only be a relatively short-term view. Warne will not be playing county cricket for ever.

So much for the batting. The England fielding is not as naturally athletic as that of some other countries. Like it or not, we are in the age of the self-made wicket-keeper who has to contribute with the bat more than he does behind the stumps. A craftsman such as Keith Andrew would be hard put nowadays to be selected for Northamptonshire let alone England, given that he was a tailend batsman. Alan Knott, the best wicket-keeper I have ever seen, better than Farokh Engineer of India and Wasim Bari of Pakistan, also set a standard for batting that has been heightened still further by Adam Gilchrist. In Geraint Jones, a cricketer from a similar mould, good enough to play as a specialist batsman, another talent has been unearthed. He should have played Test cricket sooner than he did, for Chris Read was neither a brilliant 'keeper nor a good enough batsman for Test cricket. Jamie Foster was a better prospect.

Is it an attacking or defensive ploy to have Jones in the team? Jones drops the odd catch, not least because he opts to dive in front of first slip. I have always thought that if wicket-keepers feel they can reach the ball, particularly when an edge is below shin height and hence might not reach the slip cordon, they should go for it – I tell them that they are the only paid fielders there are. England have to sort out, though, where first slip stands, in accordance with where Jones wants him. I think there is a tendency for him to be positioned a bit too wide.

An on-going debate raged in the 1990s over whether Jack Russell, a natural wicket-keeper and a useful batsman, should play for England instead of Alec Stewart, the better batsman and a manufactured wicket-keeper. One straightforward criterion decided the matter for me – Russell, who liked to stand up to the stumps to medium pacers, dropped more catches. Jones, like Stewart, will develop into a more than adequate 'keeper and will provide an all-round balance to the team. Although too high a percentage of his shots go square of the wicket, he possesses sufficient flair to score a considerable number of Test runs and relishes going for his shots. The joy of discovering him is that the tail is that much shorter, a necessity indeed in the modern-day game, in which everyone is expected to contribute.

Likewise, the spin bowler in the team should be able to bat. Fortunately Ashley Giles is as capable of making runs as Warne, particularly if he is given the room to flay the ball. There were twenty better spinners than him when I started playing county cricket but he has worked on his accuracy and bowling over the wicket into the rough. He has a good arm ball from around the wicket, which swings back in to the right-hander. If, say, he delivers 25 overs and takes two wickets for 75 or 80 runs on a flat pitch, he can be deemed to have made a good contribution. That will amount to almost a third of the overs in a day's play and enables the quick bowlers to rotate, which is what's wanted.

As far as quick bowlers are concerned, by comparison with those around in the 1990s, the development of Steve Harmison has been no less exciting than that of Flintoff. He was at a stage at which he had either to pull himself together or give up completely. It is possible to sympathise with anyone who suffers from homesickness but evidently he could envisage what he would be throwing away in terms of money as well as talent. I should imagine that when he underwent football training with Newcastle United, Bobby Robson told him just how good he could be. He possesses pace, control, nice rhythm, although he has to watch that he does not bowl too many no-balls and is not wasteful in his line or length. His action should not cause him any fitness problems. The bounce he gains through his height gives him a dangerous edge. He needs to keep up his aggression in the way that West Indian fast bowlers achieved without resorting to sledging. Although he bowled too short of a length in South Africa in 2004–05 and tried to overdo the bouncer, I do not think he was as out of sorts as was implied by the criticism he received. Too many commentators – and we return once again to the inescapable figure of Geoff Boycott – were too reactionary. Of greater significance is how Harmison reacts when a batsman such as Matthew Hayden or Adam Gilchrist takes him on.

These are exceptional strikers of a ball, given the freedom to play as they do because Justin Langer can hold the innings together. Gilchrist is the finest batsman of all the wicket-keepers I have seen, if not as accomplished a wicket-keeper as his predecessor, Ian Healy, or Alan Knott. He holds the balance in the Australian team because he is effectively an all-rounder, someone who could hold down a place as a specialist batsman. How, then, to bowl at him and Hayden? Don't allow them any width to swing their arms through the line of the ball. Tuck them up on middle and leg stump, defend the leg side and try to strangle their scoring. There is a temptation to bowl outside off stump at such batsmen and hope their extravagant driving will result in a nick to the slip cordon. That, to my mind, is not worth pursuing because they strike the ball so hard that edges will fly over the heads of the fielders to the boundary.

That said, Harmison and Matthew Hoggard, who is capable of shaping the ball in to the left-hander, hitting off stump from over the wicket, are quite up to running through the lower middle order. I rate Ricky Ponting and Damien Martyn very highly, but Michael Clarke, who made such a promising start to his Test career, still has much to learn. As the record sponsorship deal he received in Australia would suggest, he is regarded very highly, but my initial impression from watching him in 2004 during his time with Hampshire was that he should be advised about his chances of succeeding when he goes down the pitch to a competent leg-spinner such as Danish Kaneria. I would not read too much into his lack of runs in county cricket; he is not the first person to have struggled on the new pitches at the Rose Bowl.

I have a high regard for Hoggard as a very good day-in, day-out hard-working fast bowler, the type every team needs. A measure of his desire to succeed is that he was not rated as highly as James Ormond or Alex Tudor at England Under-19 level. He was never first choice and yet look at the pecking order now. Ask Hoggard to come on at 4 p.m. on a red hot afternoon and he'll run in and try his hardest. As was shown in South Africa, he needs to be given the new ball, particularly if it is a kookaburra, in order to give him every chance of making it swing. He deserved his success in bringing about victory in Johannesburg. For a number eleven batsman, he is capable of contributing to some valuable partnerships and is quite prepared to go in as nightwatchman, even after a hard day's bowling. He is a countryman, a dog walker and would have liked to be a vet, so I can readily empathise with him. Chris Silverwood, one of several effective Yorkshire bowlers, could have been no less useful had he learned to shape the ball away from the bat and not bowled so straight.

James Anderson is quite capable of bowling out every team, but I have the impression he has lost a bit of pace. He needs to keep up a consistent speed of between 83 and 85mph allied to swing and control. If he goes down to 80 to 83mph, the swing will be more of the banana kind than late movement. Like Gus Fraser and Andy Caddick and, if you like, Brian Statham, with whom he is compared, he needs to bowl regularly. He needs to play county cricket. He is a rhythmical bowler, not the kind who will benefit from a fortnight off, and hence suffered from the itinerary in South Africa in 2004–05 when there were no matches against state opposition between Tests. A full season of county cricket would not do him much harm. He did not bowl enough in 2004–05.

Simon Jones, by comparison, is a beneficiary of central

contracts. He and his father, Alan, justifiably have been concerned about the lack of pace in the pitches in Cardiff, but the pull of Wales has been paramount when he has considered moving on. When I first saw him in action at Millfield School, he was nothing more than a young fast bowler, albeit an athletic one, who had to develop greater accuracy. He still has to do so. Study his bowling analyses and it becomes apparent that he concedes too many fours. Any one over can include one ball that goes to the boundary and two indifferent balls. He must watch himself in the field and not make the kind of attempted sliding save that led to such an horrendous injury in Australia. I would not have wanted any of my fast bowlers to try to cut the ball off in that way and do not imagine the Australian fast bowlers are asked to do so. McGrath, Jason Gillespie, a similar bowler who obtains a little movement off the seam allied to bounce, and Shane Lee, who is very dangerous with the new ball because he can swing it at 90mph, are too valuable for that. I recall once writing about the case of Ashley Cowan, the young Essex fast bowler, KISS – 'Keep It Simple Stupid'.

Several England players came to the fore through A tours and, although the National Academy effectively now fills the void between Under-19 and Test cricket, I should like to see them reinstated. For one thing, every player can be included in a representative match and any emerging country should be playing against this standard of opposition or MCC touring parties and not full Test teams. The significance of having what is effectively a young England team is that someone such as Rodney Marsh, or indeed his successors at the National Academy, should be tough enough to affirm that a particular player does not possess the necessary credentials to succeed and could be checked again in two years' time to see if he is taking enough wickets or making enough runs. There is no point in choosing someone to bowl to, say, Hayden, if he is frightened of letting go of the ball. When I coached England A, I was able to inform the selectors or Micky Stewart that, whereas Hussain and Thorpe had potential, Andy Afford, the Nottinghamshire left-arm spinner, would not become a Test bowler. These recommendations were acted upon.

This would be the proper level at which to participate against Bangladesh and Zimbabwe, who have been granted full status only so as to provide further votes to tip the scales of dominance of the International Cricket Council in favour of India and Pakistan. I do not believe they should be given the same full voting rights as the founder members, who are losing their power base. The future of cricket, not of politics, should be all that concerns any country, but such are the differences that I would not rule out a split.

Otherwise Scotland, Ireland, Holland or Denmark could just as easily have been elected member countries instead. That said, I believe that for the sake of unity, Australia and England should visit Zimbabwe for one-day matches – so long as they can go in and out of the country quickly. The punitive action they would suffer from ICC if they opted out of these occasional fixtures has to be taken into account. I met Robert Mugabe and his cricket-loving bodyguard on the A tour I managed and he was friendly enough, if clearly interested more in publicity than in the game. I have also met a number of Ministers of Sport who have not shown any enthusiasm for taking decisions over moral issues in sport. I do not suppose they ever will do so and international cricket will continue to muddle along.

I N D E X

academies
  Australian 20, 45, 61
  county 174
  Essex 166, 168, 170
  National 13, 94, 189, 200
Acfield, David 47, 92, 118–19, 129,
  151, 166
Afford, Andy 201
Agnew, Jonathan 112
Ahmed, Mushtaq 45
Akram, Wasim 109–10
Alam, Intikhab 59
Alderman, Terry 129, 154
Allen, David 104, 106
Alley, Bill 111
Ambrose, Curtly 79, 80, 81, 82
Ames, Les 32, 73
Amiss, Dennis 4, 31, 36, 40, 42, 92,
  129
Anderson, James 199
Andrew, Keith 165, 195
Antigua 80, 82
apartheid 58, 137
Arlott, John 21
Arnold, Geoff 28–9, 30, 66, 87
Atherton, Michael 36, 37, 60, 62–3, 70,
  72, 73, 74–8, 79, 81, 83, 88, 91, 94,
  95, 96, 99, 100, 101, 107, 109, 111,
  112, 113, 114, 159, 161, 185, 186
  in Australia 65, 66, 69
  and Hick 68, 69
  in Zimbabwe 111

Australia 6, 11, 17–18, 19–23, 44, 45,
  54–5, 57, 58, 63, 74, 98, 114–15,
  161, 181, 186, 187, 200
  schools 44–5
  1962–3 105
  1968 17, 20–2
  1970–1 5, 17, 20, 23, 24, 25, 34, 37,
    103, 115, 124–5
  1974–5 4, 6, 25–37, 41, 76, 125–6,
    130
  1977 17, 42
  1978–9 43
  1985 18
  1989 18
  1993 54, 58–60, 61, 63, 65–6, 76
  1994–5 17, 57, 60, 65, 66, 67–8,
    69–72, 85, 109, 112, 115, 155
  2005 192
Australian Board of Control 133
Australian Cricket Academy 45, 61
Australian Cricket Board 29

Bailey, Trevor 3, 10, 11, 20, 23, 38,
  123, 144, 145–6, 147, 150, 151
ball-tampering 109–11
balls, white 110, 180
Bangalore 133
Bangladesh 192, 201
Baptiste, Eldine 128
Barbados 9, 78, 80, 81
Barclay, John 96, 107
Bari, Wasim 196

203